GERDA STEVENSON is an award-winning writer, actor, theatre director and singer-songwriter. She has worked on stage, television, radio, film and in opera, throughout the UK and abroad. She is a recipient of Scottish Arts Council and Creative Scotland writers' bursaries, won the YES Arts Festival Poetry Challenge in 2013, and the Robert Tannahill Poetry Prize in 2017. Her stage play *Federer Versus Murray*, directed by the author, toured to New York in 2012 and was published there by Salmagundi. In 2014 she was nominated as Scots Singer of the Year for the MG Alba Scots Trad Music Awards, following the launch of an album of her own songs *Night Touches Day*. She has written extensively for radio, including original plays and dramatisations of Scottish novels. Her first poetry collection, *If This Were Real* (Smokestack Books, 2013), was published in 2017 by Edizioni Ensemble, Rome, as *Se Questo Fosse Vero*, translated into Italian by Laura Maniero. A seasoned performer, she won a BAFTA Best Film Actress award for her role in Margaret Tait's feature film *Blue Black Permanent*, and is the founder of Stellar Quines, Scotland's leading women's theatre company.

By the same author:

Poetry

If This Were Real (Smokestack Books, 2013)

Se Questo Fosse Vero / If This Were Real (Edizioni Ensemble, Rome, 2017)

Inside & Out: The Art of Christian Small, with an introduction and poems by Gerda Stevenson (Lyne Press, 2018)

Plays for stage

Pentlands At War, a community play, co-written with the Pentlands Writers' Group (Scottish Borders Council Library Services, 2006)

Federer Versus Murray (Salmagundi, USA, 2012)

Skeleton Wumman (2014)

Out of Eden, a collaboration with artist Gwen Hardie (2017)

The Rime of the Ancient Mariner, an opera libretto, with composer Dee Isaacs, for the University of Edinburgh (2018)

Plays for BBC radio

Island Blue, co-written with Iain Finlay MacLeod (2007)

The Apple Tree (2011)

Secrets (2011)

Homeless (2013)

A Day Off (2015)

Room For Refugees (2017)

For children

The Candlemaker and Other Stories, illustrated by the author (Kahn & Averill, 1987)

Quines

Poems in tribute to women of Scotland

For
Jean

GERDA STEVENSON

warmest good wishes,

Gerda Stevenson

Luath Press Limited
EDINBURGH
www.luath.co.uk

First published 2018

Reprinted 2019

ISBN: 978-1-912147-32-8

The paper used in this book is recyclable. It is made
from low chlorine pulps produced in a low energy, low emission
manner from renewable forests.

Printed and bound by Bell & Bain Ltd., Glasgow.

Typeset in 11 point Sabon

For my mother,
Marjorie Stevenson –
nurse, archivist, gardener,
nurturer –
inspirational bonnie fechter

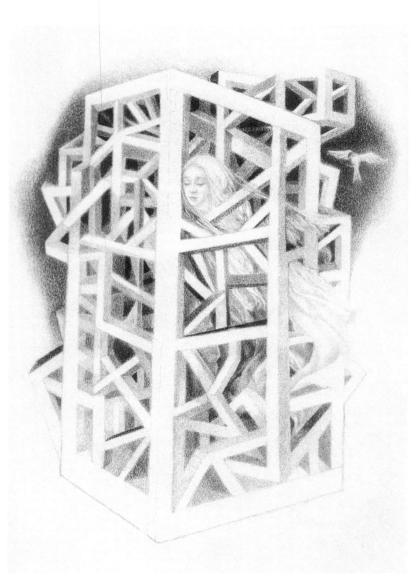

Isabella MacDuff, Countess of Buchan, pencil drawing by Anna Wiraszka

Contents

Acknowledgements

Several poems in this collection have appeared in the following publications: *PENning Magazine*; *Scotia Nova* – Luth Press; *Authors' Reading Month* anthology – Czech Republic; *Hunterian Poems* – Freight Books; *Umbrellas of Edinburgh* – Freight Books; *Northwords Now*; Scots Language Centre.com; *L'Ombra delle Parole Rivista*; scotiaextremis.wordpress.com; Dangerous Women Project – IASH, University of Edinburgh; the Gunnie Moberg Archive; Read Raw Ltd; *The One o' Clock Gun*; Elsie Inglis and the Scottish Women Hospitals – WW100 Scotland.

Thanks to: my family, friends and colleagues for their suggestions, support and patience – in particular: my parents Marjorie and Ronald Stevenson; Aonghas, Rob and Galina MacNeacail; Anna-Wendy Stevenson; Jenny Alldridge; Professor Meg Bateman of Sabhal Mor Ostaig (UHI); David Betteridge; Dr Michel Byrne; Chloe Cheeseman; Andy Croft of Smokestack Books; Lorna Davidson (former Director of New Lanark Trust); Sally Evans; Professor Marco Fazzini of Ca' Foscari University, Venice; Oriana and Maurice Franceschi; Bashabi Fraser; Simon Fraser; Glasgow Women's Library; Richard Holloway; Gwyneth Hoyle; Baroness Helena Kennedy, QC; Dolina Maclennan; Laura Maniero; Rebecca Marr of the Gunnie Moberg Archive; Dr Sarah Neely of the University of Stirling; Alex Norton; John Quinn and Professor Gina Wall of Glasgow School of Art; Professor Alan Riach of the University of Glasgow; Lesley Riddoch; Juliet Stevenson; Zillah Jamieson, Abby Richards and Ken Thomson of the National Wallace Monument's *Scotland's Heroines* project; Dr Louise Yeoman.

I am deeply indebted to Dr Jamie Reid Baxter for his generous editorial assistance and encouragement over a sustained period, which has been invaluable.

Special thanks to Anna Wiraszka for her beautiful frontispiece illustration and to Creative Scotland for their support towards researching this collection.

Introduction

She was a brilliant woman, of beauty and estate, who was never satisfied unless she was busy doing good – public good, private good... we all loved her; fell down before her; her very appearance seemed to enthral us... the noblest Roman of them all... a woman of the noblest make-up whose orbit was a great deal larger than theirs – too large to be tolerated for long by them: a most maligned, lied about character – one of the best in history though also one of the least understood.

WALT WHITMAN WROTE these words about Frances (Fanny) Wright, daughter of the Scottish Enlightenment, born in Dundee in 1795. She was a writer, orator, feminist, abolitionist, a champion of worker's and women's rights, a fearless critic of the banks and of religious institutions. Outspoken about the great pleasures of sexual passion (which she refused to equate with shame), she saw the institution of marriage as a form of female slavery. She campaigned for birth control, divorce, and property rights denied to married women. She had a play produced on Broadway and thousands flocked to her lectures. Greatly admired by Mary Shelley, she was a close friend of General Lafayette, and impressed Presidents Thomas Jefferson and Andrew Jackson, from whom she sought advice. Yet she was forgotten in her own lifetime, and is now almost unknown.

I first came upon this extraordinary woman in Barbara Taylor's fascinating book *Eve and the New Jerusalem*. I followed up with Celia Eckhardt Morris's excellent biography: *Fanny Wright: Rebel in America*. Then, in 2012, on a day off from performing in New York, I visited the Walt Whitman Birthplace Historic Site at Long Island. To my great delight, the first thing I saw on entering the beautiful museum was a portrait of Fanny Wright, prominently placed on the wall between Whitman's parents – such was her seminal influence on the great poet. He recognised in this woman a fellow trailblazer.

A year later, while working briefly in Shetland, I tried to find a boatman to take me out to the island of Mousa. I've always wanted to visit the broch there – one of several ancient Iron Age tower structures unique to Scotland, and this one still relatively intact. Mousa isn't far from mainland Shetland – tantalisingly close, in fact – but it was late October, past the tourist season, and the weather stormy. No-one would take me. So I went to Lerwick's Shetland Museum instead. There I discovered a young woman. From the moment I saw her, she claimed all my attention. Like the Broch of Mousa, she was thousands of years old, and although I was looking at her reconstructed head, she appeared to me to be more alive than anyone I'd met for a long time. I felt she could have been my daughter – same colour of eyes and hair, same ski-slope nose. Who was she? What language did she speak? Why did she die so young? She looked uncannily contemporary. Does history really separate us, or does it reveal how much we have in common? A poem was brewing...

I wrote it on the flight home, Shetland and its Broch of Mousa slipping away beneath me. I began to wonder whether this could be the beginning of something – a poetry collection, perhaps, giving voice to Scottish women through the ages, including Fanny Wright. I started ordering books. The ones I needed were often out of print. Yet many of these women I was discovering were so contemporary in their sensibilities and observations. In the utterly absorbing book compiled by her daughter, *Personal Recollections, from Early Life to Old Age, of Mary Somerville*, this major international figure of science (born 1780) reflects on environmental issues: returning to the valley of her birthplace, she is perturbed to see the River Jed 'invaded by manufactories: there is a perpetual war between civilisation and the beauty of nature'. And, in her ninth decade, Somerville writes on women's place in society:

Age has not abated my zeal for the emancipation of my sex from the unreasonable prejudice too prevalent in Great Britain against a literary and scientific education for women. The French are more civilised in this respect, for they have taken the lead, and have given the first example in modern times of encouragement to the high intellectual of the sex. Madame Emma Chenu, who had received the degree of Master of Arts from the Faculty of Science of the University in Paris, has more recently received the diploma of Licentiate in Mathematical Sciences from the same illustrious Society, after a successful examination in algebra, trigonometry, analytical geometry, the differential and integral calculus, and astronomy.

When the First World War broke out, France delivered for the female sex again – this time for Elsie Inglis, taking her up on her inspired offer of the Scottish Women's Hospitals, the first all-women mobile hospital unit. The British Government's War Office had turned down Elsie's offer with the words: 'Good lady, go home and sit still'. Nothing daunted, Elsie approached the French, and, on the 5th December, 1914, the SWH was posted to Royaumont. Its heroic work soon expanded to the Balkans, and Elsie was the first woman to be awarded the Serbian Order of the White Eagle. In Serbia, she holds the status of heroine, and is known as 'our mother from Scotland'.

Another remarkable woman who received the same award for service with the SWH was doctor and psychiatrist Isabel Emslie Hutton. In her vivid autobiography, *Memories of a Doctor in War and Peace*, she laments the potentially devastating effects of the infamous Marriage Bar, a common practice which prevented women from working in their chosen professions after they had married. In this way, many a brilliant woman was excluded from the thoroughfare and network of professional life, her career losing momentum while, as Congreve puts it, she 'dwindled into a wife'. One notable case was the artist Dorothy Johnstone, whose paintings were shown as part of the beautifully curated exhibition *Modern Scottish Women: Painters and Sculptors, 1885–1965*, at the Scottish National Gallery of Modern Art, in 2016 – a real eye-opener. The Marriage Bar was finally lifted in Scotland in 1945, having done its work in relegating thousands of women to oblivion. But the culture of exclusion still continued, as Christian Small discovered when she applied for her first professional post in the late '40s, having graduated with honours in chemistry from St Andrews University. Initially, the company she applied to was interested in the possibility of taking on this excellent graduate, until it became clear they were dealing with a woman. Christian received a letter of rejection, with the unforgettable words: 'We regret your sex'.

My priority in this poetry collection, however, is not to highlight injustices (many though there be), but rather to celebrate achievements and to explore something of the richly diverse contribution women have made to Scottish history and society. Some are well known, some less so, and others almost completely unknown. My *Quines* represent a wide range of professions and social classes – among them singers, politicians, a fish-gutter, queens, a dancer, a marine engineer, a salt seller, sportswomen, scientists and many more. Several in this collection, such as Mary Garden, Mary Slessor and Fanny Wright were born in Scotland, but made their mark abroad. Others – for example Esther Inglis, daughter of Huguenot refugees – came from elsewhere and made Scotland their home. Immigration has played a positive part in our history and continues to do so today.

From the outset I decided that all the women I included would be deceased and the poems would be monologues in three modes: in the voice of the subject, or of someone, or something, related to her. Thus, sometimes a human being is speaking, and at other times, an inanimate object – such as a novel, a bank note, a ship, or a building. There are only two poems in my own voice – the Prologue and the Epilogue.

Two main criteria have emerged in arranging the sequence of poems: the chronology of the women and that of historical events. Themes influence the order only occasionally. Initially, I placed the women strictly in the sequence of their birth dates. But as the collection developed, a story of Scotland was beginning to emerge. It seemed, therefore, that rather than sticking rigidly to a sequence of birthdays, it might be better to employ a more flexible approach, placing the women in relation to particular historical events within their own lifetimes – events in which they'd engaged, thereby throwing light on their lives, and on history. The exception is artist Maud Sulter. Because of my interpretation of her powerful photograph, *Terpsichore*, I've taken Maud out of her own era – 20th/21st century – and placed her in the early 19th century, along with abolitionist Fanny Wright and freed slave Eliza Junor.

In finding a voice for these women, I've considered the question of Scotland's three native languages – Gaelic, Scots and English. Mary Slessor, for example, was born in Aberdeen, brought up in Dundee, and lived most of her adult life in Nigeria. She was fluent in the Efik tongue and spoke with a strong Scots accent – indeed, often in Scots – as did Jane Haining, who was also a linguist. A daughter of English parents, I was born and raised in the Scottish Borders, and grew up hearing Scots spoken in my home village; but although I'm married to a Gael, and am familiar with Gaelic, I don't speak it with any fluency. So where the voices are Gaelic, I've attempted to suggest that language with a hint of its syntax. And where I quote from the women themselves, within the body of each poem, their words appear in italics.

Many of these women were deeply religious – of course, the majority of people were, for much of the recorded past. Religion has influenced Scottish society and individuals throughout the ages. In her exploration and understanding of the universe, Mary Somerville, a committed Christian, saw science and religion as entirely connected and consistent with one another. Helen Macfarlane, the Chartist revolutionary, greatly admired by Karl Marx, sees Christ as a manifestation of the democratic principle:

> I think one of the most astonishing 'experiences' in the history of humanity, was the appearance of the democratic idea in the person of a poor, despised, Jewish proletarian – the Galilean carpenter's son, who worked – probably at his father's trade – till he was thirty years of age, and then began to teach his idea, wrapped in parables and figures, to other working men – chiefly fishermen – who listened to him while they mended their nets, or cast them into the lake of Gennesaret... Do you understand now the meaning of the words: 'Democratic and Social Republic'? They are the embodiment of that dying prayer of our first Martyr: 'That all may be one, even as we are one.'

Psychiatrist Isabel Emslie Hutton comments on the theme of religion in her autobiography:

> ...children in my day were brought up on the maximum of Christian terror and the minimum of Christian love. It is indeed not too much to say that many Scottish children went through a mild conflict, which might almost be termed religious melancholia, before their first decade of life, and that some carried their guilt and fears with them into adult life.

The research process has been fascinating, and at times frustrating. The internet is a double-edged tool, both indispensible and dangerously unreliable. Take the case of Carrie Boustead, the footballer: she doesn't feature in this collection, although she almost did! She appears in several online articles and websites as the first Scottish black female goalkeeper, in the trail-blazing women's football team known as 'Mrs Graham's Eleven'. But on detailed examination, the dates didn't quite add up. I smelled a rat, and, on further digging, discovered that, in fact, Mrs Graham (aka Helen Matthews) and Carrie Boustead, who was white, both grew up in Liverpool, a few streets apart, and would have been too young to play in that first ever recorded women's international football match – Scotland v England – at Hiberbian FC's Easter Road Stadium, Edinburgh.

As the mother of a daughter who has Down's Syndrome, I'm keenly aware of the marginalisation of people with disabilities in our society. In my attempt to find a woman who represented the disabled community in some way – after phoning and emailing various organisations – I kept drawing a blank. But during a further bout of internet excavation, I discovered the amazing activist, Margaret Blackwood. In this case, as with several others, online research was essential.

Books have played the biggest part in the process of discovery. I've now built a small, precious library on the lives of remarkable women, some of whom, for various reasons, haven't made it into this collection. There are so many I could have chosen, as evidenced in *The Biographical Dictionary of Scottish Women*, an invaluable resource. My selection is by no means comprehensive – it can hardly be more than a snapshot, and, inevitably, a very personal one; nevertheless, it pays tribute to women whose lives and legacies deserve to be examined and remembered. They gathered skills, experience and wisdom against great odds, and were often excluded. The barrister and pacifist, Chrystal Macmillan, one of the organisers of the International Committee of Women for Permanent Peace, is a case in point. The ICWPP (part of the International Congress of Women) had planned to meet in Paris at the same time as the official Peace Conference was being convened at Versailles in 1919. But women delegates from Central Powers were not permitted to travel in France, so the ICWPP met in Zurich, just as the Treaty of Versailles was published. Shocked by the terms of the Treaty, the women drew up a resolution and sent a telegram to members of the Peace Conference in Paris:

> This International Congress of Women expresses its deep regret that the terms of peace proposed at Versailles should so seriously violate the principles upon which alone a just and lasting peace can be secured, and which the democracies of the world had come to accept. By guaranteeing the fruits of the secret treaties to the conquerors, the terms of peace tacitly sanction secret diplomacy, deny the principles of self-determination, recognise the rights of the victors to spoils of war, and create all over Europe discords and animosities, which can only lead to future wars.

The women of the ICWPP were not only excluded from playing what could have been an effective part in determining the course of history, their advice and warnings were ignored, at the world's peril. We cannot afford not to hear from those representing half the human race. We maun tak tent.

Gerda Stevenson
February 2018

Prologue

Reconstructed Head of a Young Woman

(Shetland Museum)

I press my brow to cold glass –
two women, head to head:
your face tilts like a ship's prow
challenging the wind,
morning sky over the North Sea
in your salt-washed cheeks
and eager, blue-green eyes.
Your hair falls like mine
from a centre parting, though holds
no trace of grey in its peat brown sweep.
Five thousand years between us, and yet
not a moment, it seems – recognition
like that spark you'd know how to strike
from stone. Thought tugs at your mouth's harbour,
a half-smile about to slip its mooring into laughter.

Your skull lies beside you, mute echo,
shell-white in spotlit stillness – every curve
and crevice mapped by expert minds:
your mask their exquisite calculation,
more real to me than any excavated bone.

Did you sleep, wake, love and weep
in the dark air of honeycomb chambers
built by shores I've only glimpsed
from plane and car – my stay too short
and anyway, my timing out of season?
I want to know you, unknown woman,
walk with you the cliffs at Silwick,

tread the paths of Scalloway, hear
your language beat the air again
with skua, scart and arctic tern,
learn your life, those days that stretched
behind your step, and (though you couldn't guess
their end would come too soon) gave you
such a fearless gaze of hope.

Quines

Nessie

The name you gave me masks your fear;
you paint my monster head so small –
pea-brain perched on a silly neck –
and give me a round, wee wifie's belly.

The real me strikes terror in your heart:
my mind broad as your kyles,
its levels layered as the Cairngorms.
My paps slope with the grace of Jura,
their nipples bright as fresh water pearls,
sleek hips fit for tender cargo.

I carry all our stories, from long before
the Romans named the Picts, and I'll elude
your sonar probes and camera clicks –
I'll only rise when you can see
beyond the surface, fathoms deep.

Sgàthach

Warrior queen of legend, and martial arts teacher, Isle of Skye;
mentor of the Irish hero Cú Chulainn, who sailed from Ireland to
train with her.

I'm a shadow, only a murmur now,
on a scattered choir of tongues,
though sunlight still splinters the waves
through my crumbling castle's arch,
like the knives I taught Cú Chulainn how to throw;
across the bay, the Cuillin leaps from where the sun
once flung its spear, black crags clawing the sky
in ragged gabbro; the hazel woods of Tokavaig
whisper the wisdom I gathered there to share
with my fledgling warriors. But my art has long
been lost – the way of patience, to balance anger
on a blade of grass in the wind, and let it cool,
till you grasp the devastation it might have wrought;
how many times, to no avail, I warned Cú Chulainn
his rage would slay his only son: 'That temper of yours,'
I told him, 'will scorch a land for many moons,
where peace might have prevailed.
Hunt down your own fear first,' I said. 'Feel the heat
of your breath on the bow-string as you pull, then
hold it, and take pause before you strike the heart
of what you do not need to kill.'

Note: Mythology tells us that the Black Cuillin mountain range sprang
from a spot on the Isle of Skye where the sun flung a spear into the ground;
and also that, as foretold, Cú Chulainn inadvertently killed his son.

Teneu

Also known as Saint Enoch, 6th century, probably pagan, later
claimed as a Christian saint; mother of the City of Glasgow, and of
Saint Mungo / Kentigern.

'Teneu!' His owl call rang from the Mother Rock – 'Teneu!'
I slipped from bed, past my father's door, rising dew
a spur at my heels, up to the whale-back summit
and our tryst: Owain, my chosen one, quite
the part in his sister's borrowed gown, curve of calf
a moonlit glimmer through a frayed seam – 'It snagged
on the rampart,' he whispered, following my hungry eye.

We slid into the Maiden Stone cleft, a perfect fit –
tender his breath, 'Teneu,' he sighed,
nuzzling my flesh below the stars.

Rowans ripen on the branch; my belly grows full;
'Teneu!' my father's wolf howl splits the air,
'For this you'll pay!' I'm whipped, and lashed
to a chariot – a death trap with no horse –
wheels rumble under my back, and gather speed
as black clouds roll; then silence; I fly
over Dunpelder's ramparts, my babe
floating under my heart – hang
on the air with a prayer to Coventina:
Hold safe this life in my womb's well.
She hears, and offers up her hidden spring,
its deep green sphagnum cloak to break our fall.
The land lies still. A hawk calls. The ropes
have slackened. I rise and walk, two hearts
drumming through my blood.

'Teneu!' My father's fear is greater now
than all his rage – his adder tongue flicks
my name, 'Teneu! I know you for a witch!
You will not live to spawn that child –
I'll have you drowned!'

We bob, spin, plunge and soar
on a million hissing knives, no oar
for guide, a doll inside a doll
inside a skin and willow shell;
Oh, Coventina, quell these waves
within and all about me,
cradle me safe to shore!

I sweat on cool sand, my mind a haze
in the dawn haar; I dream of an oak
that never grew, a red-breasted bird
that never flew, a ring in a fish
that never swam, and a swaying bell
that never rang.

The haar lifts. Sticks crackle and blaze.
A stranger tends the fire, and holds a cross
to my brow; I heave in time with the tide
that carried me here, ebbing now, gasp
my name to this man whose hand I grip
in the last arc of birthing pain: *Teneu!*

Note: Glasgow's coat of arms, linked to legends of Teneu's son, Saint
Mungo, is associated with the rhyme: 'Here is the bird that never flew,
Here is the tree that never grew, Here is the bell that never rang,
Here is the fish that never swam.'

Unn the Deep-Minded

Born Norway, c.850, died Iceland, c.900; Viking leader, also known as Aud and Audur; lived in the North of Scotland, where her son, Thorstein the Red, ruled for many years.

1

We have here all we need
to leave this land – oak and pine
for the boat, seal skin for rope,
and wool to weave a sail;
I'll not be beaten by defeat –
deep in these woods, we'll hide,
till our *knarr* is built. Now they've won,
the Cat People will lie low while winter snow
cloaks the fells and dales we once claimed
and held, but lost today.
We could have filled lochs and fjords
with blood spilled these long years;
it falls to me to lead the rump that lives.
My mother always said new shoots can grow
from a stump to sturdy limbs, till acorns drop
at last: my grandchildren must secure our line,
but not through war: change has found its time.

2

I mark the tide; we slip away at night unseen
from Gills Bay; no matter what the old laws say,
I'm captain. Our kists carry my family wealth intact.
Slaves row to my command; I've pledged them freedom –
hope spurs their oars at every stroke.

Stroma looms, then Swona; our dragon's head
bucks as we near the Swelkie whirlpool,
but I tell my crew I trust this witch
who turns her wheel beneath our keel
to grind the ocean's salt; she drives us through.

3

My granddaughters bid me farewell,
one by one, waving from Northern shores.
I've wedded them to good men –
this is my cherished plan:
from Orkney to the Hebrides,
from Faroe to my resting place
in the Land of Fire and Ice,
I'll braid for us an arc of lasting peace.

4

All is done. My grandson's wedding feast
begun: in the great hall, Celtic men whoop
their freedom with bone flute bird call;
drums summon dancers to the floor.
But for me – no more. I take myself to bed.
It's time to leave: I have here all I need –
my boat will be my cradle in the grave.

Saint Margaret

*Born Hungary, 1045, died Edinburgh, 1093; married to King
Malcolm III – Ceann Mòr / Canmore; the only royal Scottish saint,
known as the Pearl of Scotland, but among the Gaels as 'Maighread
nam Mallachd'.*

There was luck in it that day,
we thought, good fortune rising for us,
though an accident, they say:
taken by storm, she was – twice –
first at sea, driven to our shore,
then at the king's heart: Ceann Mòr
just *had* to have her for his queen.

She came from two lands – one we didn't know,
far to the East, the other we did – too well.
Cho brèagha, was the whisper of the court,
this woman more fair than any we had seen,
pale as the pearls I clasped around
her slender neck at dawn each day,
jewelled fingers spooning warm *brochan*
into blue-lipped orphan mouths
by the palace door at sunrise –
always before she broke fast herself –
giving forever on her mind.

She bore our land a line of kings,
gave us Queensferry for the pilgrims,
miracles, peace and constant prayer,
swept change through the old church
with the lovely lustre of her Roman rites.
So proud of her, our king, who couldn't read,
he had her books encased with gems and woven gold

in praise of her refinement; she held the key to heaven,
he said, and to the labour of our earthly days,
his court's guiding star in this tale of new ways
told in English from that hour she wore the crown;
for he charged us all to speak her language,
put her at ease, and willingly we did.

And now she rests with him in our Saviour's arms.
I miss her quiet radiance that filled the years.
I walked to her cave today, down by the river Ferm –
her place of solitude and contemplation;
I thought to thank her in prayer – and here's a thing:
standing there alone in that womb of rock, I yearned
for the old tongue my mother learned me on her lap,
words that once rose up from deep inside me;
but they're lost, the well is dry – it's like a fatal thirst
that can't be quenched; and I know now why
my mother called her Margaret the Accursed.

Note: St Margaret's Cave, a place of pilgrimage for centuries, can still
be visited. The entrance is through a small stone building in a corner of
Glen Bridge car park, Dunfermline.

The Dwaum

Isabella MacDuff, Countess of Buchan, 1286–c.1313, Fife; in defiance of her husband, she crowned Robert the Bruce as King of Scots at Scone in 1306, during the Wars of Scottish Independence; captured by Edward I of England, and imprisoned for four years in a cage hung on the walls of Berwick Castle.

1

Strange, the wey ye get yaised tae a thing –
the wund whuppin its braith through the baurs,
sun slingin its spears, hail hurlin its flanes,
year ower year. I dinna feel the cauld ony mair
in ma tatterwallop goon; the day, I sweir
I hae a norrie that ma limbs are growin hair,
saft, lik the down o a doo – mibbe I'll hae wings
by morn, an flichter awa...

2

Aftentimes I dwaum, aye the samin dwaum:
I'm layin my hauns on the saucrit Stane
tae gaither its pooer, layin them, again an again,
Comyn's stowen meir on the cobbles ootby,
her braith a reek in the nicht, she's champin at the bit.
Syne we're heidit North fae Lunnon Toon,
her hooves dirlin ablow an eldritch mune.

It's dawin fair when we win the Border,
tho by Scone, we're droukit wi dounfaw an swelt;
an he's there, pacin the palace grun – furrit an back,
back an furrit – Bruce, waitin fur *ma* hauns alane.

The dwaum, the dwaum, the samin dwaum,
I lay my luif, first ane then t'ither, on the saucrit Stane,
oor braw Stane that Edward daured tae rieve;
ma clan alane can croon oor nation's king.
I hae the pooer; on his pow I place the gowden ring.

3

Cages are lang-kent tae me;
lang, lang afore noo, fae the day
I ettled tae flee the bield, a lowp
in ma spang, howp in ma hert,
a hale rowth o time aheid o me;
but claucht an hapshackled
in a union biled in hell, aa wrang,
a line leal tae Edward, thirled
tae yon auld Comyn carl, agin ma will.

He hoasts an he hirples,
The weary day lang,
Maids, when ye're young,
Niver wed an auld man...

I hae a hoast in ma lungs the day –
berkin like a dug – an unco hirple an aa,
sae I'm telt by yon wumman wha casts
the brock tae me – cauld kail an parritch
that maks ma kyte bowk.

4

A skimmer o licht on the waves ablow.
Scotland tae the North, England tae the Sooth.
The samin mune abuin us aa, that hus nae care
fur stane or nation, croon or king. I'm hingin heich
amang the sterns; am I dwaumin? The baurs
o ma cavie hae fell awa, the down on ma limbs
gies a fissle, a reeshle, ma feathers prick,
ma wings are spreid oot wide, they lift me,
slaw and strang intae the glisterin nicht.

Queen o the Bean

*Mary Fleming, 1542–1581, Scotland; relative, childhood companion
and lady-in-waiting to Mary Queen of Scots; on **Uphaly Nicht** – the
Feast of Epiphany – in 1563, Mary Fleming was the lucky one to
get the piece of traditional King Cake (Black Bun) with the bean
concealed in it, and so was 'Queen of the Bean' for the night.*

Yon wis a ploy! In ma mindin fur aye.
It stairtit at breakfast, wi cake – she couldnae wait.
We were sat up in bed thegither (ever sin I claucht
thon cuif o a French poet hid in her chaumer, fired up
fur hoochmagandie, we'd slept side by side);
'Noo, ma douce wee cuz,' says oor Lady Queen,
gien me the ashet, 'tak a bite o Black Bun,
an let's see if ye'll beir the gree!' I sink ma teeth
intae crisp pastry crust, syne hinnie faulds o moist daurk –
raisons, cinnamon, almonds, citrus, ginger, as if
the essence o thae gifts the Three Kings
brocht tae Christ are fluidin ower ma tongue's buds;
and then it comes – the haurd, leamin surface
agin ma gums – the bean! An her lauch like licht
fills the mornin: 'Ye will be Queen this Uphaly Nicht!'
says she, awready oot o bed, rakin through her kist
o treisurs – they're skailin tae the flair in a skinklin spate.
'I'll hae ye geared up sae braw, ma Mary dear,
ye wull cherm the hale court – a glisterin spreet
o Christmastide ye sall be, nae maitter that Maister Knox
hus bainished it frae the almanac; I wull mak ye
a merrie Phoenix that wull rise afore us aa!'

Och, ye shoud hae seen me, tho I say it masel –
I wis braw! She hud me happed in a siller goon,
Orient stanes threidit through ma braidit hair,
dreepin frae ma broo, ma halse, ma paps –
ma hale form a veesion in amethyst an jade,
emerant, amber, topaz, an a sash o sapphires, blue
as the dawn ower Bethlehem; bangles o gowd,
pearls like snawdraps, rubies reid as Rizzio's bluid.

Bluid. Ower muckle o't hus syped awa
doon the years sin syne, thae daffin days
o licht-hertit ploys. The warld is grey an mirk,
a wanlit place withoot a braith o colour tae its face,
nae feastin noo, nae dancin, guisin, liftin o the hert
in sang; oor anely solace fur the saul is kennin we hae
lauched thegither, lauched sin we were careless bairns
in a blurr o bluebell wids on haly Inchmaholm; lauched
as lasses, at the lottery o it aa, the castin o the die:
Queen fur aiblins hauf a hunder year,
or ae ferlie nicht, fur juist a blink.

The Abdication of Mary Queen of Scots

After the painting of the same title by Gavin Hamilton; Mary
Queen of Scots, born Linlithgow, 1541, died Fotheringhay, 1587;
imprisoned in Loch Leven Castle, 1567, where, on 20th and 23rd
July, she miscarried twins, and was forced to abdicate the day after.

Tak ma croon, an dinna fash –
aa yon wis ower fur me lang syne.
Ye needna glaum at ma silk goon
wi yer coorse nieve – I'm nae threit;
I'll sign yer muckle scroll, dae whit I maun,
past carin noo; thae last three days ma flesh
an saul hae wandert shores o hell-fire, dule an daith:
twa bairns I cradled in ma wame aa through the months,
sae douce, o Spring an Simmer, slippit cauld an stieve
intae the dowie air o Leven's grey stane waas,
claucht frae ma jizzen, an burriet ootby, wi nae prayer,
fur aa I ken, an nae sang, twa scraps o heiven,
aa ma howp in their twin licht smoorit noo,
tho milk's aye buckin frae ma breists unner ma lace an steys;
an I couldnae gie a fig fur yer fouterin laws,
sat there, scrievin yer Latin clatters o queens an kings –
O, I could run rings roon ilka yin o ye in Greek an aa,
as weel's ma bonnie French, but ye're naethin, naethin noo,
juist ghaists; an, och, Mary, Mary Seton, last
o ma fower leal ladies, dinna waste yer tears
on gien up a bittie gowd an glister, haud ma airm
if it helps, but dinna, dinna greet fur *this*.

Nine Haiku for Esther Inglis

*Born France 1571; moved to Scotland in early childhood, daughter
of Huguenot refugees; lived most of her life in Leith, Edinburgh,
where she died in poverty, 1624; considered by King James VI of
Scotland (I of England) to be the finest calligrapher in the land; also
an embroiderer and miniaturist portrait painter.*

Goose and crow quills scratch
a tiny patch of parchment,
giving flight to words.

I paint myself – not
vanity, necessity:
a lord may hire me.

A ragged man sells
seed pearls from a burn; I stitch
them to books for kings.

Honeysuckle scrolls,
thistle spikes and fleur-de-lis
twine with damask rose.

Like a butterfly,
I inhale from harebell cups
the tang of blue ink.

I was King Jamie's
'most exquisite writer in
this realm'. Now debt stalks.

My constant husband,
dear daughters and son, I fear
my steady hand fails.

From the Lord goodness,
from myself nothing. Till death
I will chart his praise.

All creation dwells
in a leaf, bird, bloom or word
in my Maker's book.

A Dochter's Dreame

Elizabeth Melville, Lady Culross, c.1578–c.1640, Fife; poet; the earliest known Scottish woman writer to be published in her lifetime, her Calvinist dream-vision poem, 'Ane Godlie Dreame', appeared in 1603; wrote to her son on his sister's death that she – i.e. her daughter – was 'hevylie trublit in mynd and body. Pryde wes the cheif thing that trublit hir, and the greving of hir deir mother, as she callit me then. Bot efter a soir battell, she gat a happie victorie, blissed be God. Nou she rests in the arms, all tears are wyppit away.'

Oh, mither dear, I dreamed a Dreame:
this fecht wi life hud left me deid
wi dule; I dreid that your esteem
I crave, is turnt frae gowd tae leid –
your howp in me is nocht.

It wis your ain Dreame, whilk ye wrocht
wi wurds like jewels, in a beuk,
the samin Dreame ye read tae me
in bairnhood; and, wi care, I teuk
your ilka wurd tae hert.

I fear the vaige I hae tae chairt
frae this hersh warld, whaur I hae failed,
through vainity, and pride (as ye,
aft-times, hae warned and richtly railed).
The voice was yours, I sweir,

in ma Dreame – sad and solitaire,
like a bird on a bare brainch, threap,
threapin me tae haud fast, white'er
suld pass – ice, fire, or warse: the dreep,
dreepin stang o misdout;

but I stumblit, could nocht cast oot
a laithly fear o aathing – shame
o masel, yer dochter wha suld
gie hersel to Him, whaes true name
is aa that can endure.

Torment, ma paiks; there is nae cure
fur lost sauls. Mither, tell tae me
aince mair yer Godlie Dreame, that I
may nocht be brunt in hell – oh, gie
ma saul the will tae pray!

The Killing Times

Margaret Wilson, Wigtown, 1667–1685; Covenanter, executed
by drowning, during what was known as The Killing Times, for
refusing to swear an oath declaring James VII as head of the church.

'Margaret, dear,' a wumman cries
frae 'mang the gaithert thrang, 'Juist say it –
juist say thae wurds: God save the King!'

The stake's no twa fit ower the watter noo,
the tide risin, lickin ma sister's chin.
I wade in, up tae ma breists, ma jaw chitterin,
appen ma mooth tae speak, but my vyce
is steikit; I glaum at the hem o her goon,
its grey faulds bellied abuin the waves,
but she doesnae see me – her blue een raised
tae the lift. She's singin her saul oot, a psalm
she learned me as a bairn, ilka note ringin clear
ower the wide Solway Firth.

A man scraichs ahint me – him
that tied her tae the stake twa-oor syne –
clauchts ma airm in his muckle nieve,
and waps me back. I plowter tae the shore,
sabbin mair saut nor whit's aboot me;
but he's lowsed the raip, and humphs her
like a deid seal tae the machair,
draps her there 'mang gress and flooers
flidderin careless in the wund. Her lungs souch –
there's braith in her yet. 'Juist fower wurds,'
the wumman ettles again, in a whisper noo:

'God save the King.' But ma sister's saul is leal –
thae words wunna pass her stane-cauld lips,
fur aa their soun wull gie her life.
'Damned bitch!' sneists the man, 'Gie the oath!'
But she'll no dae it neethur. He grabs her hair,
drags her doon tae the sea aince mair.
Slaw, wi baith airms, he heezes her heich
abuin his heid, fur aa the warld tae see,
like he's beirin the gree; slaw, sae slaw,
he mairches wi her, yont wave efter wave,
till the tide's up tae his bull-thick neck,
then casts her oot like a stane.

'Columbine' Cameron

Jean Cameron – also known as Jenny – born Glen Dessary,
Knoydart, c.1695, died East Kilbride, 1772, where a memorial has
been erected to her memory; heroine of the 1745 Jacobite rising.

I look North to Glen Dessary –
home – though can't return
to its devastation, always North,
to the 'Glen of the South-facing place',
my back turned on those false tales
that fanned about me like redcoat wildfire,
growing flanks, battalions of lies
sweeping over the border, on and on
(never falling back, as we did at Derby),
gathering heat till they licked the heels
of Fleet Street, and danced in the footlights
of Drury Lane – a play named after me,
would you believe! *Columbine Cameron,*
Britannia's nemesis, sprite of hell,
nightly rousing rebellion
in Scotia's frozen wastes –
such was the reach of my fame,
in this high-stakes game of war;
it seems our masters need a whore,
a bitch to blame – and better still
if she has 'the vulgar Highland tongue',
a 'she-cavalier' with claymore.

I've become in others' eyes
so many versions, all perversions
of my self. But there's none
among them can tarnish the truth
of that August day on summer's cusp,

leaves turning to gold by the shores of Loch Shiel:
I led my clan to Glenfinnan – three hundred men –
our hope with the Standard rising high.

Hauf-hingit Maggie

Margaret 'Maggie' Dickson, Musselburgh, 1702–1765; a salt-seller;
hanged for alleged murder of her illegitimate child; she strongly
denied the charge.

Daith is wappin whan it comes – like birth;
I ken – I hae warstled throu, an focht wi baith.
She wis blue, ma bairn, blue as the breist o a bird
I seen oan the banks o the Tweed thon day; then grey,
aa wrang, the naelstring windit ticht aroon her neck;
I ettled tae lowse it, aince, twice, but it aye slippit –
ma hauns couldnae grup, ma mind skailt
frae the jizzen fecht, ma mooth steikit:
no tae scraich, no tae scraich, lat nane hear...

I stottert oot, doon tae the watter, thocht tae douk her
in its cauld jaups, but ower late. I laid her quate
in lang reeds, achin tae hae a bit basket tae float her oot
like Moses, aa the wey tae England an the sea,
gie her a deep grave, ayont kennin; but they fund her,
still as a stane whaur she lay; an syne me,
wannert gyte agate Kelso toon. 'Murther!'
they yaldered, 'Murther!' like dugs.

Embro Tolbooth's a dowie jyle. An mercy? Nane they gied me
at ma trial – the verdict: hingin. The duimster slippit the towe
ower ma heid, drapt the flair – but I'd lowsed ma hauns,
I grupped thon raip, aince, twice, thrice at ma thrapple –
I'd dae it this time! The duimster duntit me wi his stick,
dunt, dunt, an the dirdum dinged in ma lugs,
'Clure the hure! Clure the hure!' Syne aa gaed daurk.

A chink o licht. The smell o wid, warm – a cuddie's pech;
ma een appen. I lift ma nieve, chap, chap oan ma mort-kist lid,
chap, chap! A scraich ootby, a craik o hinges. I heeze masel, slaw,
intil ma ain wake, at the Sheep Heid Inn. Fowk heuch an flee:
'A ghaist, a bogle, risin fae the deid!' I sclim oot, caum.
The braw brewster gies me a wink, hauns me a dram.
I sup lang the gowd maut, syne dauner back tae life, an hame.

Note: Maggie Dickson was charged with, and condemned for, neonaticide,
i.e. murdering her newborn child, under An Act Anent the Murdering of
Children, introduced to Scotland in 1690, later known as the Concealment
of Pregnancy Act. This is the same crime for which the character Effie
Deans, in Walter Scott's novel *The Heart of Midlothian*, is condemned to
death. In 17th and 18th century Scotland, if a woman had concealed her
illegitimate pregnancy, and the baby was discovered dead, or the birth
reported and the baby disappeared, the mother was often charged with
murder. The basis of Scottish Law is Roman. Therefore, in Maggie's case,
once the Court's judgement had been carried out, she was deemed to have
paid her dues. Having survived execution, she was regarded as dead in law,
and, unlike in England, could not be re-hanged.

It's Aye Sang wi Me

Carolina Oliphant – Lady Nairne, 1766–1845, Findo Gask,
Perthshire; singer-songwriter; throughout her life she adamantly hid
behind the nom de plume: 'Mrs. B of B'. Many of her songs were
long assumed to be by Robert Burns and Niel Gow.

I bide in twa leids, blen wi baith,
leared lang syne: ain frae The Auld Hoose –
ancient Gask (redolent of heroes' tales,
rich with relics of Jacobite fame),
t'ither frae the Clathy fowk doon the Strath,
sang in their darg that dirls through ma banes
and dings in ma hert – it's aye sang wi me.

Love is hard-won, acceptance the key,
a surviving girl child, I wished I could be
the son my father waited long to sire;
I'd walk among trees he planted and named
for my buried sisters, stroked by their leaves,
rocked by their boughs, songs in their whisper
from the Land o the Leal – it's aye sang wi me.

But ma sangs are ma dern – they hae tae be:
I dinnae want praise – yon's vainity; oor Lord
sent us here fur tae dae his guid wark,
no tae muse on oor ain; yet I canna but beek
in the kennin I hae that Maister Niel Gow
and Burns himsel hae ruisit the airs
o Mrs. B. o B.! It's aye sang wi me.

Note: 'The Auld Hoose', and 'The Land of the Leal' (the latter being a
term for the afterlife) are songs by Lady Nairne.

Self-Control Promotes Herself

Mary Brunton, novelist, born Orkney, 1778, died Edinburgh, 1818; her novel, Self-Control, *was greatly admired by Jane Austen, whose first published work,* Sense and Sensibility, *appeared a year later, with a similar theme.*

They say 'Don't judge a book by its cover'
and I say, they're right! From Page One
my title's subverted, my heroine overcome by her lover,
a libertine for whom she's on fire, and almost undone –
there's no doubt about it, she's in dire straits.
This is no tale of buttoned-up protocol,
my chapters race with passion-driven mates –
she's barely a heart-beat, a whisper away, from being his moll:
he only has to appear at the gate, and she melts, would be
in bits were it not for her faith and another love-sick,
loyal paramour, number three in the triangle: he can see
warfare in her soul, but patiently waits, time tick-
ticking away, as she's lost to him, across the ocean,
locked up in the wilds, with no-one to hear her cries.

Mine is a wholly modern yarn, no false emotion,
no romantic froth – my heroine a working woman, who tries
to sell her wares, and succeeds, who dares
to take control – doesn't wait for the fairy-tale knight
to sweep by on his milk-white steed; she snares
the moment fate casts her way, that split second of light
in the nightmare, and shoots down the rapids
to freedom from a madman's chains; there's not a breath
of tinkling tea sets and tete-a-tete, nothing vapid
in me, or outmoded – I'm a page-turner, no shibboleth –
read me and I swear I'll thrill you to death!

In Her Ninety-Second Year

Mary Somerville, born Jedburgh, 1780, died Naples, 1872;
mathematician and astronomer, for whom the term 'scientist' was
coined; recipient of numerous international honours; an island
in the Arctic and a crater on the moon are named after her; she
predicted the discovery of Neptune.

My mind, of a morning, never fails to whet its blade
for a duel with Euclid (and ofttimes with Newton,
for good measure) – five hours of algebraic cut and thrust
fairly sets me up for the day! My naked eye can still count
each thread of a fine cloth, and memory holds intact
the passage of years; but the fact is, my footsteps falter,
and though my hearing lacks precision, it tunes
into a persistent, shrouded whisper – father's mantra,
when his fleet's departure neared:
'Soon I must expect the signal for sailing.'

'The child's a savage!' he declared, home from sea
one summer, to find me shamefully unschooled;
I preferred the open book of Burntisland's shore
to alphabet and abacus – shells my first stardust.
Dispatchment to school, my torso clamped
in deportment steel, only deepened my feral flaws.
I still revel in every sepal and petal of a wild orchid,
and a swallow's flight across an evening sky will ever
transcend the geometry of Venus in her transit path,
though I'll regret, when the final signal sounds, not yet
to have known earth's distance from the sun.

But now I mind on it, only give me
by moonlight for my last song

the celestial tinkling bells
of Lake Como's silken fishing nets,
and I'll speed in all glad haste to meet
our Great Ordainer with no regrets.

Captain Betsy Miller's Fareweel tae *Clytus*

*1792–1864, Saltcoats, the only woman whose name has ever
appeared in the British Registry of Tonnage as captain of a vessel;
eldest of eight children; worked as clerk to her father, Captain
William Miller, with whom she sailed regularly; took over as captain
of the* Clytus, *aged 46, making a great success of the family business.*

I've been a husband tae ye, niver a wife,
aince ma faither's ship, but lang ma ain,
the *Clytus*, a Trojan – true tae yer name,
ma braw snaw, wi yer twa masts,
biggit anew frae an auld man-o-war,
bow like a beak sneddin the swaws,
ma maik, ma marra, siccar an strang.

Myntit, we were, tae fare thegither,
storm-steidit or caumed, through aa wather,
jyned at the hip – till noo. I could awmaist greet
tae leuk oot the winnock an see ye there,
anchored ootbye, as if bidin yer time,
waitin fur me tae gaither ma docht.
But it winna be, fur life has brocht me
tae its hinner-end, a hantle o days
I wudnae troke fur douce wifely dues.

O, we hae kept the faimily afloat
wi siller, peyed aff the debt ma faither left,
an muckle mair – year in, year oot,
tae the Emerant Isle an back again, a leal crew,
oor cargo, Scots coal an Irish lime – daurk an licht.
I wudna sit by the sill till caunle flames
blawed a sauf airt, we'd be heidit awa,

a braig tae the faem that daured tae tak
ma brither Hugh; an tho, sin syne, we aye hae sailed
wi ma windin sheet, yon oor he drooned
I hecht I'd tak the helm an live.

It's lyin here in the captain's kist, ma linen shrood.
Winna be lang noo till I'm happit in its saft faulds.
I'm yare fur this, ma last vaige – sister Hannah's staunin by,
she kens the raipes: ye're in guid hauns.

Note: During a storm Betsy famously said: 'Lads, I'll gang below and
put on a clean sark, for I wid like to be flung up on the sands kin' of
decent. Irvine folks are nasty biddies!'

Terpsichore Reflects on Her Master

*After a photograph, entitled 'Terpsichore', by Maud Sulter, born
Glasgow 1960, died Dumfries, 2008, of Ghanaian and Scottish
heritage; artist, photographer, writer and curator; her work is held in
a number of collections, including the Victoria and Albert Museum
and the Scottish Parliament.*

Your ebony muse, you call me.
The kind, I take it, that can't refuse
her master's bidding? I'm your morning's sport,
a clandestine delight, got up in your wife's gown
so sheer white, I dazzle my own eyes.
My stomach heaves at her sweat whiffing
from the seams, and the fetid pomade
of apples and lard wafting from her wig,
as you slip its tail round my ear and neck.
And what's that – the glittering shard
you place in my hand – a tiny slice
of your stocks and bonds, my slave wage
for this caper? 'A lucky charm,' you whisper,
'a talisman to fire your steps, my Terpsichore –
dance now, give me a black tarantella, bring me
crashing to the rocks on waves of my desire – undo me,
as your Siren daughters (when you spawn them)
will undo so many men.'

And so it begins – you beat the tambourine.
I'll prance for you, but I'm only marking time;
one day – let it not be far away, let it be soon –
you'll be dancing, and to another's tune.

Note: In Greek mythology, Terpsichore was one of the nine Muses,
goddess of dance and chorus.

Fanny Wright Meditates on Mary Shelley's Death

*Frances (Fanny) Wright, born Dundee, 1795, died Cincinnati, 1852;
lecturer, writer, freethinker, feminist, abolitionist and social reformer;
first female editor of a newspaper,* The Free Enquirer; *the first
woman in America to publicly oppose slavery.*

The news is through – sweet sister, you are dead.
You kept the lock of hair from this tired head
since that day we met, I'm told – said my curls,
and thoughts, were like your husband's, so a churl
I'd have been to deny you! We were young
then, and America was freedom's lung,
I believed, when I asked you to sail with me
to this land of the great Liberty Tree,
but your heart was moored to old Europe's shore.
'Child of love and light', may your spirit soar
and steer me onward, lead me through this mire
which clags and drags my soul to a hell-fire
of self-doubt: that I have wedded the cause
of human improvement, and without pause
staked my reputation, my whole fortune,
my entire life on a wild, blind auction,
bidding for an illusion, and lost all.

You knew my birthplace, Mary, and drank deep
from the well of Enlightenment, no sleep
for our restless minds till democracy
becomes reality, not prophecy;
yet that longed-for state is more distant now,
it seems to me tonight, than the bright plough
high above Cincinnati's candle-light.
Since you breathe no more, who cares what I write

or think, and why should they? Who can resist
the weight of law and religion, the fist
of finance that cloaks its blows with sweet bribes,
until our brave new world and all its tribes
are subjugated, lost and tyrannised,
by cool monopolies that brutalise?

No longer can I hire a hall to spread
the word to thousands, as I used to – 'Red
Harlot of Liberty' they daubed me, scared
of joys I freely proclaimed when I shared
the supreme truth that flesh touching flesh, in
or out of wedlock is pleasure, not sin –
'High Priestess of Infidelity'! Shocked
when I railed against vile slavery, mocked
for exposing the lethal marriage trap
which snared me in the end, the deadly slap
that silences, and strips the female sex
of all her assets – sad, abandoned wrecks
strewn on a shore without the God we're taught
will save us; but he never lived – I fought
to lay bare *that* lie: man-made opiate –
yet another glittering potentate.

But, Mary, *I* have lived! – ridden bareback
o'er the prairie, slept by a lonely track
and found Nashoba – place that held my dreams,
though they failed, like most of my cherished schemes;
Many times I've sailed the North Atlantic,
valued great men's friendship – the romantic
General Lafayette, who strove for change
with old Jefferson; but now, I'm estranged,
no community, no society –

eke out my days in quiet poverty.
Those I've loved are gone, and now you too,
who held your mother's torch, the flame that grew
with every step we took to forge a world
pledged to the common good; but my heart's thirled,
without the strings to tie me to the cause;
someone else who knows Utopia's flaws
yet can hold to that faith, must clasp the flame,
carry it forward without fear or shame,
proclaim and sing the body politic
free and whole, a change so deep it's seismic,
wider than the seven seas, to carry
justice in a tide to all shores, Mary –
the old, buried song in a new, young voice,
a tender force, that bids us listen, rejoice,
throwing out a spark of hope this drear night
in the lonely loss of your shining light.

Notes: 'Child of love and light' is a quote from Percy Bysshe Shelley's
dedication to Mary in his poem 'The Revolt of Islam'.
The end of the first stanza is an adaptation of Fanny Wright's own
words – the epitaph on her tombstone in Spring Grove Cemetery,
Cincinnati, Ohio: 'I have wedded the cause of human improvement,
staked on it my fortune, my reputation and my life.'

Demerara

Eliza Junor, born Demerara, 1804, died Fortrose, 1861; daughter of Hugh Junor, slave owner from the Black Isle, and an unknown mother, probably a slave, or a 'free coloured' woman; won a prize for penmanship at Fortrose Academy.

I've learned my letters well – my copperplate masts and sails
flow across the page, like the ship that carried us here,
my brother and me, to our father's land, the Black Isle
of white people, where I'm glad no cane grows;
my mother always said I had a way with words –
Demerara – River of the Letterwood, its banks of trees
with bark like hieroglyphics, a whisper in my ear from birth:
Demerara, Demerara… I wish she'd lived to see my prize
for penmanship, that I could tell her we are well, and freed,
that we don't heed the taunts of *half-breed, octoroon,
mulatto, quadroon;* the dominie's wife says *tawnie* –
told me she'd seen some in Cromarty too,
had heard rumours there were others come to Inverness
and Tain; and, saving present company, wasn't it a shame
that Scotsmen didn't refrain from relations with slaves?
She was pouring tea, and her spine stiffened in her corset
when I declined the sugar. 'But it's *Demerara*,' she crooned,
'It'll make you feel at home,' and spooned it into my cup;
I watched the gold beads – 'hybrid jewels',
my father calls them – melt in the peat-brown pool.

Note: In adulthood, Eliza became the single parent of an only child – a daughter, who grew up to be a governess.

Seeing Red

*Helen Macfarlane, born Barrhead, near Glasgow, 1818, died
Nantwich, 1860; Chartist revolutionary, admired by Karl Marx as a
political commentator and essayist, she was the first translator into
English of* The Communist Manifesto, *published in* Red Republican
*magazine, under the nom de plume of Howard Morton, her identity
as translator not revealed till 1958.*

I've always seen red:
Christ's hands on the cross –
He bled to show us, mother said,
that we are all divine, and no-one
may enslave another.

Workers' hands in the family mills, steeped
in vats of red madder and bullocks' blood,
raised high like flames, waving our wealth:
Turkey Red bandanas they'd laboured to create –
a crimson tide against redcoat dragoons
riding in to break the strike.

Red raw my sisters' eyes – how they cried
when the mills went down, our brothers forced
to sign away the family fortune, all we owned,
our gracious home – its stair carpet a scarlet artery
under the skin of Royal Crescent's cool façade.

Red the robin's breast on a winter branch,
my spirit soaring, Christ's gospel with me as I board
for Vienna; and red the anger I found there; a fire of hope
within me when the monarch fell, a tumbling imposter –
the advent of a new idea preached in ancient Galilee.

Bright red the joy when my babe was born, red hot
the scalding pain at the flutter of her failing heart, my ear
to that hidden ruby buried deep, as she slipped into Christ.

And red, red my thoughts that flow with His tidings,
onto page after page: how can we leave a single soul to die
by inches in squalid lanes and gutters, making slop shirts
at tuppence apiece, while another is swathed in silk?
We must grasp the meaning of His words, His dying prayer
that *All may be one, even as we are one.*

Note: The last stanza includes a transposition of Helen's own writings
published in *Red Republican*.

Òran / Song

Mary MacPherson, known as Màiri Mhòr nan Òran / Great Mary of the Songs, 1821–1898, Isle of Skye; Gaelic poet, singer-songwriter, and bard of the Highland Land League; falsely accused of and imprisoned for theft.

I lay inside her,
a buried spring
rising, drop by drop,
the colour of her days
in every hidden trace –
the moorland's green and gold
waving summer innocence
in the careless barefoot time,
before the long trail of exile
gathered like ash, and only
the bone-white bleat of sheep
fretted the air; I lay there,
silent but rising, for fifty years,
darkening at the black fear
preached from the pulpit,
churning at the lies spread
about her stealing a slice of silk
from her dead mistress –
the shame of it, as if their ilk
hadn't thieved her people's land,
those masters of the sleek tongue
she wearied of, that tried
to silence her own; buried still,
I was, but rising higher, till
the iron bars of the prison cell
closed on her; and she stood alone,

listening, as though the metal clang
rang through her flesh and bone,
summoning me, and I broke
from her throat in anger's flood –
a well of song that flowed
and never faltered
in its fearless cry for justice,
carried down the years.

Mary Slessor Takes St Paul to Task

*Born Aberdeen, 1848; raised in Dundee; from childhood worked
in the jute mills; died Nigeria, 1915, where she was a Christian
missionary, promoter of women's rights, protector and adopter of
children, mostly twins, believed by the Efik people to be possessed
by evil spirits and left to die after birth; fluent in their language, she
was trusted by the Efik people, who called her 'Ma'; a passionate
pragmatist, and challenger of orthodox theology and thinking.*

Wives submit tae their husbands, ye say?
Na, na, Paul, laddie! This will no do!
Ilka morn oor guid Lord shows the way:

man, wumman, bairn, for *aa* we maun pray
in equal measure; ilk ain is due
the same rights. This I winna betray.

Men condemn twin bairns tae die in clay
jaurs, here in Calabar – I ask: who
daurs tae mak sic laws? His saul will pay!

My God wudnae demand I obey
ony man's decree that wisnae true
tae common sense, frae whilk I'll no stray.

My sex doesnae mean I canna lay
cement, mix it like a parritch brew;
Oh, Lord, let it set! is aa I say,

and it does, sae ma bairns sleep and play
withoot parasites and the cauld dew
hermin their young flesh, baith nicht and day.

I hae traivelled faur and choose tae stay
'mang fowk wha never kenned font nor pew.
Roof, flair, medicine – nae fine array –

are whit's needit here tae do away
wi mortal fear, that begets voodoo,
stalking like a leopard fur its prey –

women, aye women, and bairns tae slay.
Sae, Paul, laddie, I'll no preach whit you
telt the Ephesians; come whit may,

I'll show Calabar's braw men I hae
a sweeter power than they, and strang too;
wives submit tae their husbands, ye say?
Na, na, oor guid Lord shows the way.

Note: 'Na, na, Paul, laddie! This will no do!' These are the words
written by Mary Slessor in her bible, the pages of which were covered in
her own marginalia, often challenging the text.

Janie Annan Slessor Keeps Vigil

1882–1918, Nigeria, of the Efik people; birth name: Atim Eso; she was Mary Slessor's beloved daughter, adopted as a baby, a twin whom Mary saved from being slaughtered; carer and teacher, Janie was known as Mary's right and left hand woman. They visited Scotland together several times.

You are leaving us, Ma;
your breath, once fierce as a leopard's,
wavers, weaker than a kitten's now.
Abassi, sana mi yak, you say.

When you're gone, Ma,
I'll be only half myself again,
as I was when you found me –
my twin dead; you made me whole.

We are harmony and counterpoint,
you and I, we speak each other's tongue
to a double divinity –Abassi and God,
who are one to us, the way light needs dark.

Abassi, sana mi yak, you say.

I've always known two sides
to everything – born a slave, but free
now – Scot free, I like to say, bound
to you, my other half, for aye;
our symmetry the perfect blend
of white and black, your skin
pale as the powdered milk
you brought back for our bairns
that time – sprinting miles through

teeming rain to get it – mine
dark as the Calabar night
that carried you home;
our eyes two seasons of a mango leaf, yours
green with hunger to keep us fed, mine
brown as the deep pool of patience you teach.

But you're leaving us, Ma;
Abassi, sana mi yak, I hear you say.

When will we again see snow on Balkello Hill,
and gulls like spears above the Tay?
Don't leave us yet; there's still so much
to share, to build – how will I fill
my empty half, the void? Breathe, Ma, breathe,
you've done it before, hauled yourself up
like Lazarus, from The White Man's Grave;

not this time, though:
Abassi, sana mi yak, you pray,
Oh God, release me,
Abassi sana mi yak.
And you slip away.

Notes: The Efik words 'Abassi, sana mi yak' (Oh God, release me),
were the last Mary Slessor spoke as she died.
'The White Man's Grave' was the name given by missionaries to
Calabar, where, unlike Mary, most white people died within a few
years.

Horsehead Nebula Speaks

Williamina Paton Fleming, astronomer, born Dundee, 1857, died Boston, USA, 1911; received numerous international honours, including the Guadalupe Almendaro medal from the Astronomical Society of Mexico for her discovery of new stars; her name was eliminated from Harvard's list of astronomical discoveries, denying her credit for discovering Horsehead Nebula.

There I am, bucking my head below Orion's belt,
free rein in that constellation's fiery dust,
riding the stellar waves for millennia, unnoticed, till
a woman with eyes like burning stars takes one look,
has me harnessed, measured, catalogued, and tamed.
I'm proud to be groomed with such exquisite care
by one who can do it all – a maid, she was,
at the professor's kitchen sink, until he saw
her quiet gift for seeing light with a precision
that far outstripped his Harvard team of men;

and then, the men come in. I'm claimed
as their discovery, and named: 'Grim Reaper,'
'Black Knight of the chessboard,' they say,
failing to notice I'm a mare.
They make me want to leap
from this photographic plate,
leave it miraculously blank,
and take her with me, my lady of the stars
who found me first – we'd race
the heavens together, gallop across light years,
stream through Zeta's glittering rays, bareback,
all along the Hunter's belt, from Mintaka to Alnitak.

Scotland Celebrates 3-0 at Easter Road

*Ethel Hay (goal), Bella Osborne and Georgina Wright (backs), Rose
Rayman and Isa Stevenson (half-backs), Emma Wright, Louise Cole,
Lily St Clair, Maud Riweford, Carrie Balliol, and Minnie Brymner
(forwards), wearing nickerbockers in the style of the Rational Dress
movement, played and won the first recorded women's international
football match, Scotland v England, Saturday, 7th May, 1881, Easter
Road, Edinburgh.*

The wind was against us – but wasn't it ever?
We had all to play for, and nothing to lose;
we kicked off with gusto, no matter the weather,
two thousand, the crowd, their jeers couldn't bruise
our spirits; red stockings and belts a kindling flicker
across the turf, then flashes of fire, flames fanned
by self-belief, we were bonded as one, slicker
than our English sisters, that day; we spanned
the field, every inch covered, Ethel hardly required
in goal – but when her moment came, oh, the spring
in her fearless lunge to save – the whole team fired!
We surge forward, and hear someone sing,
a lone voice, at first, *Daughters of Freedom Arise,*
then more and more: *Yield not the battle till ye have won!* –
our striker takes possession, her mind on the prize,
Lily St Clair, talk about flair! – a meteor cast from the sun –
dancing and dodging, she blazes to the box, and bends
the ball in – a goal for Scotland! We weep and cheer,
Scotia's Eleven makes history, sends
a message to the world: have no doubt, we are here,
scaling the heights, new horizons in our sights
and the ball is rolling for women's rights.

My Birth in Her Hands

After a Beaten Metal Panel, of that name, by Margaret Macdonald;
born Tipton, 1864, died London, 1933; an influential artist, whose
work became one of the defining features of the Glasgow Style. The
panel was exhibited in Vienna, 1900, now part of the Hunterian
collection, Glasgow.

Painstaking, this making of me,
meticulous, slow (no tricks here,
no god to pluck me from a male rib):
heated, cooled, tapped and teased
from a blank sheet of cold metal,
the tang of tallow and resin rising
from the labour bed of black pitch.
Who'd have guessed I lay there
all the time, invisible till revealed,
naked and complete, waiting to be born
with my twin babes, each held
in lily lips stemming from my navel?

I am all female, a dreaming dancer balanced
on one toe in the birth canal, ready to enter
through its rose-studded gate into the light
of a new century, bearing hope's freight
in my prayerful hands.

Skull

Isabel Emslie Hutton CBE, born Edinburgh, 1887, where she later studied medicine; brought up near the Ochil Hills; died London, 1960; doctor and psychiatrist; awarded the Serbian Order of the White Eagle for services with the Scottish Women's Hospitals in WWI; a trailblazer in mental health; worked privately at a time when the Marriage Bar made it almost impossible for women to practise their professions.

I'd entered the graveyard after church,
my thoughts leaning from Genesis towards
Darwin's take on events, when the spade
broke your rest among my ancestors;
I feared you might be retribution, or even a curse,
worms churning the earth through clogged eye sockets;
but my friend the gravedigger only laughed:
'Tak him! He'll be mair use at yer studies
than moulderin here in the bane-thrang grun!'

The Sabbath air under the Ochils brewed
with coming thunder, my mind with dread
of parental censure, so I wedged you in a cleft
above the burn, and left you to the elements.
All night, through lightning flash, my pillowed head
filled with you, a skull inside a skull.

You hadn't budged an inch from your post,
that storm-washed dawn. Rain had scoured you
to pristine white; your benign smile a sure sign
that no transgression had occurred –
you were ready for service in another life.

From the shadows of my haversack,
your mandible flings its jaunty grin
into Auld Reekie's streets, a salvo
at the lowering legacy of Knox,
and a silent rally to the fearful.

You've given me a head start;
I'm getting to know you –
the perfect pyramid of each petrous apex,
the melancholy slope of your lacrimal bones,
your entire compliance in anatomy class,
when we sawed off your vault to view the interior
that once housed a whole world.

Diva

Mary Garden, born Aberdeen, 1874, died Inverurie, 1967; opera singer – world-renowned in her time; the first to create many leading roles in new operas, including those by Debussy, Massenet and Prokofiev.

I am granite: like the city that bore me,
I glitter. My notes transmit
the mythic lustre reflected in the hush,
the gasp, the roar of all who hear;
to sing is my heart's desire. I will not
be broken, nor tied to any man.

'Ne partez pas!' they cried in Paris,
before I sailed for New York,
'Ne partez pas!' rose petals cast from the gods
by a thousand craving hands.

With my long golden locks – a shining harvest
from the daughters of Brittany, cropped at my command –
I am, and ever will be, the *Mélisande*
Debussy barely dared to hope for,
diva of his dreams, the voice to die for,
and how I have died!
Again and again, perfecting the act
beyond all artifice. Who can withhold
belief in me when I reach the threshold
of death's mystery? The final note
floats from my soul in a rising arc,
a gleam of threaded breath
fading into devastating silence.

Rest Time in the Life Class

After a painting of that title by Dorothy Johnstone, born Edinburgh,
1892, died Bodelwyddan, 1980; artist and teacher; taught at
Edinburgh College of Art from 1914 until she married in 1924,
and was forced to resign, due to the Marriage Bar; elected as an
Associate of the Royal Scottish Academy, 1962.

I'm good at cat-napping, resting from the pose;
the murmur of learning drifts around me,
while I float off for a spell; but today – well!
There's something in the air – the grapevine drops
its fruit in my ear: Miss Johnstone's to be wed!
I pretend not to hear – a model's task, after all,
is to be mute, a purveyor of mystery beyond the flesh,
and in any case, Miss J's in the room; but this is history,
or the end of it – a gloom descends. I raise my eyelids
an undetectable sliver: Belle adjusts my charcoal outline,
while Kay, with an audible shiver, as if there's been a death,
leans into her, and whispers: 'Can it be true?'
Belle nods. Our thoughts converge on a straight line
that can't be erased: the Marriage Bar –
another good woman consigned to the grave of wedlock.
Her teaching days are done, and she won't be cycling solo
along summer byways either, with canvas and paint-box
strapped to her back. 'Today is forever blue and grey,'
sighs Belle, 'and so this painting will be too.'

Helen Crawfurd's Memoirs in Seven Chapters

Born Glasgow 1877, died Dunoon, 1954; political activist,
suffragette, and Red Clydesider; one of the founders of the Women's
Peace Crusade; also founded the Glasgow branch of the Women's
International League for Peace and Freedom; a founder member of
the Communist Party of Great Britain.

1

A tang of yeast along the street, bread
in my father's bakery, rising like prayers
from the dusty hands of aproned bakers,
white angels at dawn; in the Bible I like
Queen Vashti best – *she* wouldn't stand for it:
only sixpence to go to the fair, my brothers
a shilling each, just for being boys. *Damn!*
I cry, and fling the glittering insult at the floor.

2

The toil of oil and soot-black shipbuilders,
traipsing home at dusk to bow-legged bairns;
I pray that change for them will come –
the whole world is theirs by right;
I marry a man of the cloth, threefold my age,
who preaches care; I take St John to heart:
may his truth be known that we must love
the brother we have seen as much as
God we have *not* seen, or else we lie.

3

Christ could be militant and so can I –
he whipped the money lenders from the temple,
flung their coins at their fleeing heels; His whip
in my hand when I shatter the eyes of buildings,
where blind men sign women's fate; it flicks
beneath my skin, as I'm pelted with putrid fruit,
and through my mind in the cells of Duke Street,
Holloway and Perth, an urgent spur
to keep my jaws clamped tight.

4

I wore black for my husband and mother last year,
and wear it still, and will, for the bairns, barely born,
dying in squalid single ends. I'm on the march
with Mary Barbour's army – cards
pinned in windows, stating terms:
RENT STRIKE WE ARE NOT REMOVING.
Here, in our Second City of the Empire,
where a fanfared judge steps from his carriage
at the High Court, our ranks are ready for his bailiffs,
with warning bells and flour-bag missiles in every close.

5

Men flail and choke and bleed in mud and gas to gain
a yard of land, then lose it with a thousand lives;
I'm on the march again, Crusade for Peace,
join forces with MacLean. In a Glasgow hall,
the organ thunders patriotic strains, the Provost
takes the chair, and Miss Pankhurst's there,
once dubbed 'Queen of the Mob', she's changed her tune:
enlisting men, pinning their guilt with white feathers
stolen from our dove, pressing women to munitions,
Britannia's clarion call stoking Europe's fire
and denying equal pay. I leap to the table: *Shame
on you, not so lovely lady Christabel,
Shame on you!* I cry.

6

I balance like a bobbing doll
on the deck of a fishing boat,
dodging Norway's police.
A cargo ship booms and looms
through smirr; I scale its hull
on ropes, my black dress
wagging a wild farewell
to those bold Viking boys.
If it takes this to reach Moscow
and Lenin, I'll do it.

7

I walk along Dunoon's West Bay; the shingle slips
like a slow song as the tide slackens to the Clyde;
the years flow back with every wave: Berlin,
where I address ten thousand; the general strike,
raising aid for famine-stricken souls by the Volga.
And Connolly, courtesy itself when I gave him
that message at Liberty Hall – the eve of Irish revolution.
But now I'm letting go on this sleepy rim of the world,
though folk awoke and rose here too, I'm told –
reclaimed their common land. Tea-time.
Must get to the Co-op before it shuts.
Why don't they sell the goods that you'd expect
of such a movement? I'll write about it to the press tonight.

Note: Helen, a pacifist, was incensed when Christabel Pankhurst
suspended suffragette action and supported the British Government
by actively recruiting young men to the army during WW1. Helen's
unpublished memoirs are held at the Marx Memorial Library in
London.

The Scaur

Ethel Baxter, born Cummingston, Moray, 1883, died Elgin, 1963;
business woman, brains and engine behind the world renowned
Baxters food company.

I didnae ken whit hit me
till it stottit aff me, and brak
like shrapnel fleein aboot the flair –
ma ain slate, the dunt o't, stane tae bane,
bluid atween ma breists, sypin through
ma rived sark. 'That'll learn ye,'
spits the dominie, smoothin his goon,
like he's dichtin his hauns clean o the deed,
'that'll learn ye how tae coont!'

I'm fleein hame,
greetin, haudin a cloot
tae ma rauzit breist, saut tears
scaudin, thrashin ma wey
through simmer gress,
wild straeberries crushed
at ma heels, the scent
o their sweet bluid risin,
melldin wi ma ain,
sookit in wi ilka sab.

I hae been scaured, but I hae learned tae coont,
an muckle mair – nurse tae the man I mairriet,
wha hud the grace tae lippen tae ma ploys:
I biggit a fortune wi ma forethocht, brocht us fame,
sold yon wild, crushed sweetness o the blue Cairngorms
tae aa the airts, gaithert and set in jaurs
stampit wi the faimily name.

Oor men at war, I buckled to, stoked the bilers,
hitched up ma skirt and sclimmed the rafters
tae quate the pulley-wheels scraichin fur ile;
and ae nicht – I'll mind it aye! – made three tonnes
o blackcurrant jeely, ma belly full as the moon wi bairn.

And aa the while, ablow ma buttoned sark,
yon scaur a leamin flane aimed at ma hert,
ma merk, a hecht tae masel:
I'll no be whupped intae stour.
I'll thole ilk wap life dings, staun strang,
mend, mak and thrive.

Ma Ain Country

Violet Jacob, 1863–1946, county of Angus; novelist, poet, essayist, short story writer, and botanical artist; travelled widely abroad; her only child, a son, died in WW1.

I hae tae be here, noo I'm aa ma lane,
the anely airt that hauds hert-brak awa,
the ae merk on this braid yird I've stravaiged,
that keeps the slaw days hale, till they come
fu circle, frae cradle intil grave.

It gies ma saul peace in the hauf-lit oor –
drawn tae ma door by the cry o geese –
tae staun quate, and slock a deep waucht
o the gloamin – the snell braith o green moss
droukin ma thochts, till the constant tick
o the wag-at-the-waa ahint ma back is lost,
and yon stoondin pyne – aa ma mindin o the Somme
that reived ma son – is smoorit, fur a while;

ma eye taks up a traiveller, whustlin doon the brae,
a wraith in the still air, and I think on the life, braithin there.

Elsie Inglis Prepares for Her Last Journey

*Born India, 1864, died Newcastle-upon-Tyne, 1917; doctor, and
suffragist; opened a maternity hospital (The Hospice) for poor women,
and a midwifery resource centre; founder of the Scottish Women's
Hospitals, which sent out medical teams of over a thousand women to
Belgium, France, Serbia and Russia during WW1; the first woman to be
awarded Serbia's Order of the White Eagle.*

So, I am going over to the other side.
The secret beast I thought I had the beating of
through sheer will – this canker that divides
by stealth and multiplies – has taken hold.

Only three weeks past, as Arctic ice
clawed Archangel's port, I hauled myself
up a rope ladder, to the ship's deck,
a fluttering fleck on the vessel's flank
in frozen air. I'd soon be home and rested,
instruments prepared – hooks, clamps
scalpels, saws – ready to set out afresh
with my women's team, to heal men's wounds;
but not this time, it seems –
I'm going over to the other side.

I'd return to Serbia, if I could,
give thanks to old comrades.
I'd drink a long, cool cup
from the fountain they built there,
those blessed men, in battle's lull,
to honour us, above the Crkvenac spring,

where, in sun and moonlit flash of gunfire,
my women, saving lives, proved
what's plain as day: that we are equal –
daughters, sons, husbands, wives.

So many battles still to fight,
for votes, for wages, health and peace;
but mine are done, the hidden war
beneath my skin almost won.
'Its just an onward journey, the last
we take,' father said before he died.
Another ladder looms. Thought dissolves.
I'm going over to the other side.

Note: Elsie Inglis' last words: 'I am going over to the other side.'

Justice, Persons and Peace

*Chrystal Macmillan, 1872–1937, Edinburgh; known as the Scottish
Portia – politician, barrister, suffragist, feminist and pacifist; a UK
representative at, and organiser of the Women's Peace Congress,
convened at The Hague, 1915; an organiser and signatory of
the telegram sent by the International Committee of Women
for Permanent Peace in 1919 to the leaders of the official Peace
Conference at Versailles, objecting to the terms of the Treaty.*

The meaning of *justice* is our refrain –
if half of humankind is erased
from its scales, the word can hold no weight:
its essence ever bears a twofold freight.

Those who make our loaded laws,
say only *persons* can participate
in shaping the governance of state:
by common concord, the Lords maintain,
a person is de facto male! Thus they relegate
half the value of yet another word
to the same obliterated fate.

And what of the single syllable – *peace*,
that renders those who make it
blessed? So strong, yet misconstrued
as weak, violated at Versailles
by vengeful victors, who deny
its power to release the world
from future war; the one word
women called for, in congress
at the Hague, that syllable
whose meaning must not drop
so slow it won't be felt or sought;

hear this: in the name and face
of justice, we are persons, half
the human race, and will advance
our urgent plea for peace –
we will persist.

The Red Duchess

Katharine Stewart-Murray, Duchess of Atholl, 1874–1960, Edinburgh; first Scottish female Member of Parliament; Scottish Unionist Party MP for Kinross and West Perthshire, 1923–1938; the first woman to serve in a UK Conservative and Unionist government; resigned the Conservative Whip in 1938 in opposition to Neville Chamberlain's policy of appeasement of Adolf Hitler, and to the Anglo-Italian agreement; was then deselected by her own party, who dubbed her the Red Duchess.

I could have said 'I told you so'
but it's hardly good form,
and, in any case, Guernica says it all.
To give four thousand lives safe haven
here on Britain's shores, and stem
the flow of children's blood,
makes me human, it doesn't turn me 'red'.
Why would I comply with a party line,
let common sense lie down and die?

I could have said 'I told you so'
but *Mein Kampf* said it all,
and to make sure, for those who
couldn't read between the lines,
I commissioned its true
translation. How could they doubt
the ill intent that marched
like jack boots over every page,
the coming of Europe's darkest night
spelled out in black and white?

I could have said 'I told you so'
but the dead silence
of six million says it all.
Appeasement? So bland a word
could never hold itself upright –
I'd rather resign than touch
its breath. I wouldn't be its crutch.

I could have said 'I told you so'
but facts line up to tell their tale,
stand on each other's shoulders;
no matter how high we build the wall
they'll stare at us from the parapet
through time's eye, speak for themselves,
and say it all.

Jane Haining

Born Dunscore, Dumfriesshire, 1897, on a small farm; died
Auschwitz, 1944; Church of Scotland missionary; matron in the
girls' home of the Jewish Mission Station in Budapest; the only
Scot to be officially honoured for giving her life for Jews in the
Holocaust.

A wind wi hinnie braith – a walcome guest –
blew in the day tae Auschwitz frae the West;
it mindit me on hame, insteid o war,
brocht me closer tae ma Makker than afore.
The visit was aa ower in a blink,

but lang enough tae smoor the rank stink
o burnin flesh, and gie me gowan braes
in Dunscore wi ma mither, simmer days
o bairnhood when we learned by hert that faith
is only love, and never hate; and daith,
tho seemin fell, a wey o makkin hale
this gift o life we maun tent withoot fail.

Aa ma bairns I ken will go tae heaven,
and I am number 79467
fur lovin them – stampit wi tattoos
fur mitherin Hungary's orphaned Jews,
forced tae stitch *Jude* stars ontae their claes,
jaloused o bein a spy by oor faes
when they fund me greetin at the task,
but I wis never ane tae weir a mask –
dissembling wad hae been tae brak the vow
I made at hame, when Europe wis alowe:

tae return tae Budapest and be there
for ma bairns: *If they needit me sair
in sunshine, they'll need me mair in daurk.*

Yon hinnie wind is gaen, and aa is mirk;
men scraich orders, gas pipes hauch and hiss,
bairns whimper faur aff fur a guidnicht kiss
I canna gie them – we maun weep oor lane;
yet *We hae kenned love* is oor sweet refrain,
and like menorah branches bleezin bricht,
we cairry in us oor great Makker's licht.

The ss *Bonita* Praises Victoria Drummond

Victoria Drummond, born Errol, 1894, died East Sussex, 1978;
Britain's first woman marine engineer; awarded the Order of the
British Empire and the Lloyd's War Medal for Bravery at Sea.

I'd never been known to exceed a speed
of nine knots, a reliable plodder, you might say,
plying the North Atlantic – that's how I saw myself
(freighted with porcelain clay, that calm Sabbath day) –
nine knots, and no more, till the Luftwaffe roared
out of nowhere and *she* took charge:
bombs fall, I'm a bath toy, tossed on a wave's wall,
machine guns blaze from the scarred sky,
the lagging blasted like powder puffs
in my engine room – my main water pipe
split like a straw; but she kept her head,
though oil haemorrhaged a black jet into her eye,
no time for greaser and fireman to balk
at orders from a woman, it's clear to me
she's the one to trust – when you're out on a limb,
it's sink or swim – at her command I give my all,
and before they know it (the whole crew
can tell from her smile), I'm doing more than twelve,
dodging away from battle in a zig-zag tango
with Captain Hertz, Hungarian style!

The exam board failed her – those official men –
thirty-seven times, again and again,
till they had no choice but to let her in,
the only one who could coax me from nine to twelve,
the woman who loved to churn butter as a bairn,
the patience it takes, keeping wrist and elbow
powered to the task, till white turns slow to gold.

The River Kens Nancy Riach

Nancy Riach, born Motherwell, 1927, died Monte Carlo, 1947;
described as the finest swimmer in the British Empire.

She's steppin barefit, comin ma way
ower simmer gress – see her kilt sway
wi the sauchs; she's keepin a caum sooch –
lauchs wi her freend, twa quines, threidin
in and oot o sunlicht aa alang ma banks, till
she staps, slips aff the kilt, and stauns still
in her plain black doukers, fur aa tae see –
nae falderals, nae fuss; she tucks her tousie mop
unner a cap, gies me a kennin look, nae maitter
the cameras, and a hunner een, or mair,
o fowk wi faimilies lookin oan, wha aye wull say:
'Thon efternuin in the sun we forgat the war –
we were there – she showed us how it's duin!'

She sclimbs the widden steps, rigged up heich
abuin me, walks slaw tae the board's rim,
braw shouthers set fine, ilk lang limb
paised; we're made fur ane anither:
a keekin-gless baith – she sees hersel
in me, I ken masel in her, yon pooer
ettlin tae be lowsed; she rises on tiptae,
I haud ma braith, and she's away –
a birlin bird, whirlin through the lift,
aince, twice, then – fleet as a flane –
scoves intae me, a glent o flesh in the licht.

The Penny Pledge

*Ena Lamont Stewart, born Glasgow, 1912, died Ayrshire, 2006;
playwright, librarian, medical secretary and receptionist at the
Sick Children's Hospital, founder member of the Scottish Society
of Playwrights, and Scottish League of Dramatists; her play* Men
Should Weep *is listed by the Royal National Theatre as one of the
hundred greatest plays of the twentieth century.*

I was the promise she made to herself
as a girl – placed in her palm by a brother,
who saw the worth of a tale she wrote.
She'd lift me to the light from a musty drawer –
a silent pledge – turn me over, heads, tails,
King George, Britannia, tails, heads,
two sides, one voice; but where was her own,
that could speak up for weans with rickets,
and their trauchled mothers, those shawly women
who slogged to feed and clothe them, pay the rent,
flogged by drunk men in Glasgow's single ends?
All through the Depression, and another war,
on library or hospital shifts, her mind
would slip me out, and polish me to a lustre,
renewing the old vow;

till that night, in the hush of plush velvet stalls,
watching actors strut their hour, silver tongued
platitudes tinkling from a cocktail-time play,
she knew my service was done,
and raged home in red-hot revolt:
Life! Real life, she swore would fill her stage,
as her characters pulsed from pen to page.

Note: 'Shawly' was Ena's own coinage, describing the impoverished
women of the Gorbals, who typically wore shawls.

At Miss Eardley's

Joan Kathleen Harding Eardley, born Warnham, 1921, died Killearn, 1963; artist; her extraordinary output was created in just fifteen years before she died of cancer; celebrated for her portraits of street children in Glasgow, and for her landscapes and seascapes of the North East coast of Scotland.

'Away oot and play!' says Mum, and we dae –
nae fun dodging aboot unner her bunions.
Best place when it's chuckin it doon,
or if oor brothers are gien us jip,
is ben the big room at Miss Eardley's;
through the close, up the stair,
chap on her door, and she lets us in –
turpentine kickin its stink up yer nose
gies yer snotters a rare tang!
See the gear she has in there –
a mug, like Dad sups in the pub,
but this yin's frothin wi brushes – no beer –
and a cheese box fae New Zealand, wi a lamp
stickin oot like a crane doon the Clyde –
no packed wi cheddar, like it says on the side –
wish it wis – I could fair go a creamy slice;
paint splats like dolly mixtures aa ower the flair –
wish they were – and drippin fae tins; piles ae boards,
and canvas stacked at the waas; the day, though,
she's drawin us wi sticks o chalk on sandpaper,
rough as a cat's tongue; I'll no mind the time it takes –
she likes a blether, and so dae I, chance tae tell her the news:
the break-in doon the bakers, how they wur flingin pies
at the polis; and meantime, ma bum, numb
wi the cauld, will thaw oot by her stove.

'Admiral of the Bering' Recalls Alaska

Isobel Wylie Hutchison 1889–1982, Edinburgh; botanist, film-maker, writer, artist and intrepid Arctic explorer; awarded the Mungo Park Medal, 1934; vice president of the Royal Scottish Geographical Society; Fellow of the Royal Geographical Society of London.

I sold my ball gown to a chambermaid at Nome –
after all, 'when in Rome!' What use could tulle
and jewels be to me, cadging a lift on the gallant
ten-ton *Trader*, hunkered on my bunk,
as she sliced through ice to Point Hope?
Gone for me the foutering fuss of women's frills:
free just to be, to roam the rim of the Arctic sheet,
at ease among men.

I'd gained Anvil's summit before we sailed,
and from her tundra slopes plucked gold –
not the diggers' kind – specimens to be pressed
between paper leaves: snow-white boykinia,
primula eximia, and golden potentil,
a farewell blaze before winter set in.

At Wainwright I looted with Inuit
the ribs of a drifting ghost – who knows
if her rusted hull still rides the floes?
I froze my finger on the shutter-release
in minus 63, painted the glittering Endicott peaks,
and got snowed up for weeks with Bolshevik Gus
in his driftwood hut on a sandspit. 'I'll treat you,'
he pledged, 'like a lady,' and true to his word,
rigged up a screen for my modesty;
outside at night the dog team's breath
rose crystalline on the freezing air,

while, happed in parkas and eiderdown,
we'd debate without rancour the existence of God,
though proof – as if needed – was pulsing above,
in the sky's green harp.

My old bones must be rime-ringed now,
and full of snow, crumpled in this wheelchair,
hooked fingers leafing through memory's maps.
'The first white woman, no doubt,' Gus said,
'to reach Demarcation Point on dog sled,'
clicking my camera on the laughing length of me,
two nations straddled by my long, lean legs!

The Flyting of the Red Shoes and Blue Shoes

Moira Shearer, born Dunfermline, 1926, died Oxford, 2006;
internationally renowned ballerina and actress, famous for her starring
roles in the legendary ballet film The Red Shoes *and in* The Man Who
Loved Redheads, *in which she dances the Charleston in blue shoes.*

Redder than madder, or that sweet apple
the sleek adder made Eve pluck, we allure,
we beguile, stitched in style by a cobbler
with a gargoyle smile – a fiend who's out to kill,
and, for him, we will;
we lead her, bleed her, dance her down to death.

Sky blue, high blue forget-me-not heels –
we know the steps to take, alive to your wiles –
we challenge you with a Charleston beat,
sweet clarinet and a balalaika thrum:
she won't succumb;
we tease, cajole, but the lady's in control.

She's *ours*, we have her, all wide-eyed,
like a child craving a fairground ride; she slips
into us in a blink – heavenly fit,
she's on the brink of bliss, light as a moth,
she spins and flits;
we lead her, bleed her, dance her down to death.

But see how we release her artful wit –
that saucy kick, the deft wrist flick,
the divine disdain in her shoulder shrug,
the tilt of her chin, the tug – never smug –
of her cool restraint;
we tease, cajole, but the lady's in control.

We'll turn the heat on your slick, blue beat,
scorch her feet with searing violins,
flesh, bone and marrow, toe to flaming skull,
we're the pair to triumph with lethal flare,
breath of hell, each step of the stair
we lead her down, and bleed her, all the way to death.

Clamour your colour as loud as you will,
we infuse her with life, you cannot kill
the smoulder, the thrill, the cool blue burn
in the pin-point angle of her ankle turn;
only once in a rare indigo moon
will you see such grace – her body flows,
it simply knows how to pace the space
between syncopated notes: heel-toe, toe-heel,
we tease, we cajole, she's in control, and the band –
the whole house – they're down on their knees,
begging the lady: 'Encore! Reprise!'

Anna Buchan's Obituary

Zoologist and geologist, born Rosehearty, Aberdeenshire, 1897, died
Aberdeen, 1964; curator of Marishal College Museum, Aberdeen, and
Elgin Museum; writer of scientific articles.

Yon wumman wis somethin else – I mean,
the heidline they prentit in the paper yestreen
when she'd peched her last, didnae gie us a clue!
Ma granddochter breenged in fae the college – she's aye fou
o aa kinna by-ordinar faks that leave me ahint,
(parteecualar noo ma myndin's tint!) –
appearantly, says Susie, yon wumman kenned aa about yird,
an whit's burriet in it: fossils – like the rig-bane or fit-dunt o a bird,
an aa kinna gear – quaichs, ashets, bynes fae lang syne –
she howked oot a wheen o them atween the railway line
an Elgin road – mind, whaur the auld cley pits
yince wur warked? (Ma brither's buits
are still clarted wi thon); an there's naethin she didnae ken
aboot lamps – tillies, cruisies (like I yaised tae burn ben),
yin fae reid cley, says Susie, fae the Nile,
thoosands o year syne, fair fantoush in style.
In stourie museums she'd scance an leet ilka bit thing,
nae maitter whither tocher o pauper or king.
An she kenned awthing aboot thae mountains o ice
afore beasts were born, could luik at a slice
o yird an gie its name, date an place
on oor planet – she wisnae juist a pretty face.
An here's Susie's pint – she's beelin, oor lass,
this is the heidline that cam tae pass
abuin her obituary, the braw wumman, bless her:
'Widow of an Elgin Hairdresser.'

Mairi Anndra Gives Thanks to Margaret Fay Shaw

Margaret Fay Shaw, born Pennsylvania, USA, 1903, died Isle of Canna,
2004; folklorist, musician and collector of The Folklore and Folksongs
of South Uist *(1955), a significant book in its field; she learned Gaelic,*
living for almost five years with two native speakers – crofting sisters
Mairi Anndra and Peigi MacRae – in South Uist.

She blew in like a wind with a dance in it,
a load on her back – an Irish harp from New York,
and a box with an eye, a *Graflex* she called it, that stretched
its neck at you from folds, black and heavy as a *sgarbh.*
She learned our land, the sea, the sky, our names
for different clouds, how to cut seaweed with a *corran,*
to turn a *ploc* of peat with a spade, the time of year
for every chore; and she listened to our words
that we'd lost the writing and the reading of –
the patience of her, to learn our tongue – wrote down
our tales and prayers, the one I gave her
for the Smooring of the Fire, when Mary and her Son
and a white angel will watch all night at the door;
she took our songs to her ear and made them skip
from her fingers in lines along the page, the sound of our days
she placed there, with all her care, the look of us too, caught
in that eye, for ourselves and the world to see.

And when she came with those pages made into a book,
not one word wrong in the four corners of it,
a golden ship sailing on that blue cover, bright as a summer sea,
we cried to hold our lives in our hands.

I am Jennie Lee's Open University

Jennie Lee, born Lochgelly, Fife, 1904, died London, 1988; MP, political activist, Minister for the Arts; architect of the Open University, initially named by Harold Wilson as the University of the Air.

My wee bastard, she'd whisper, stroking the White Paper
that had my life laid out before the faithless Members,
there's plenty want to see you dead in my waters,
but I'll be mother and midwife, and you will thrive!

We were made for each other, long before she knew it:
daughter of Lochgelly – coal and leather –
families broken by the General Strike,
the town whose slit-tongued tawse
whipped bairns' palms in bleak schools,
exporting the weapon tae aa the airts,
inert strips of tanned hide, buffed to a shine
and proudly stamped with their maker's name.

Widowed by sixty, and nothing to lose,
she gives me her all: *Only the best*
is good enough! she declares, my champion
in Parliament's hallowed halls,
a challenge to their gilded ranks.
'Hope and hokum!' they howl. 'It'll never catch on!'
Dad wheels into her memory, on his bike
from Fife's mines, laden with laundry and food
to keep his lass at her studies in the capital; through me,
she swears she'll honour him, and Hardy's Jude –
his unbearable fate – lift the have-nots from obscurity
by releasing knowledge like caged birds into the open air.

And look at me now, her only child,
the *wee bastard* she dared to nurture –
how I've grown!

Note: 'Tawse' – leather strap, also known as 'The Lochgelly', after the
town where it was manufactured – Jennie's birthplace; used throughout
Scotland for punishing school pupils, until 1987, when its use was
banned by law; reference to Thomas Hardy's novel *Jude the Obscure*:
Jude was prevented from going to university due to the social class
into which he was born. Jennie said that this novel was 'one of the
formative books for me when I was a young student – the struggle for
self-education in citcumstances of poverty'.

All It Takes

Margaret Blackwood MBE, born Dundee, 1924, died Edinburgh,
1994; campaigner for disabled people's rights; her lobbying, inspired
by Megan du Boisson, resulted in the 1970 Chronically Sick and
Disabled Persons Act, leading to the introduction of benefits such as
mobility and attendance allowances.

'Learn to knit,' they said, the stale air
thick with the syrup of pity
dripping about my wheelchair.
I used to leap upstairs, two at a time,
more deer than girl, till pain
scorched my tendons, and the years,
like my limbs, wasted away.
'Or make lampshades,' they'd say.
I tried the watchmaker's trade,
and failed – time trickled through my fingers,
cogs and wheels faltering, miniature pinions,
barrels and ratchets scattered to the floor
in fragments of rage.

Yet all it takes is a scrap of news, a lifeline
buried in the small print – someone out there
like me, but she's not going down:
Megan du Boisson has a plan;

time becomes an oasis, no longer a wasteland:
I'll not wait to die, as they predict, a bedridden heap,
in that vamped-up poorhouse at Logierait,
where ghosts stir under the wallpaper,
and whisper their plea to a careless world:
Are we a dirty word?

I'm leading the protest down Princes Street –
wheelchair battalions spinning like clockwork
at dazzled cameras in the sun. Trafalgar Square
next, if they won't hear our cry: *We exist!*
I'm riding the way for change.

What a Voice

*Lizzie Higgins, 1929–1993, Aberdeenshire; traveller, fish-filleter,
singer and tradition-bearer; daughter of renowned traveller singer
Jeannie Robertson; Lizzie never sang publicly until in later life, after
her mother's death, when she made many recordings.*

She learned me in her wame,
ilka note tirlin doon tae whaur I lay,
like a bird faur aff in a daurk glen,
or a bell, dingin slaw throu watters deep –
ma mither's sang.

Time's the thing, bidin yer time – I couldnae reive
the shine fae the barrie star oor Jeannie wis,
couldnae hae her sang while she lived,
but it beat throu ma bluid, haudin me hale
whan the scaldies sconced me sair at the schuil –
radge, I wis, wi hert's care, fleein oot thae gates
wi their black airn clang; I'd no be back, I swuir.

Syne ma first day fish filletin: I'm tae be 'initiatit' –
the notes come swallin up, silent, like a siller shoal
afore ma een, as I'm dragged tae the grun,
an they try tae strip me nakit. But I whup oot ma knife.
Daur ye! says I – this time, I'll no be humiliatit –
*Daur ye touch a threid o my sark an I'll gut
ilk ain o ye bangsters, I'll hae ye mutilatit!*

'The fastest knife alive' they cried me,
crooned fur filletin a ton o fish in a flash –
the glent o ma blade wud blin ye!
An ma lemon sole: warks o art –

the King o Ethiopia traivelled tae see fur himsel!
I'd nae need tae sing fur ma supper
aa throu thae years, tho I could;
but no till it wis time.

Dawin braks on the day, a thrang o fowk
aa gaithert in her memory; the lang green gress
growin ower her grave; her sang swalls up
an oot fae me at last, tae rax her, ilka note
tirlin doon tae whaur she bides on t'ither side
o time, the sang she learned me in her wame,
an I hae wings noo, like that swallow high,
what a voice I hear, it's ma ain, like the voice
o ma mither dear, what a voice,
what a voice I hear.

Note: The last stanza pays homage to the great (anonymous) folk ballad
'What a Voice', also known as 'Blackbird', which is sung by Lizzie
Higgins on Martyn Bennett's groundbreaking album *Grit*.

Margaret Tait's *Portrait of Ga*

After a short film of that title by Margaret Tait; 1918–1999,
Orkney; pioneering experimental film-maker, poet, short story
writer and doctor; 'Ga' is Margaret's family's name for grandmother.

Mother – I need to get you in the can, I say,
your cheekbones cutting the light, hair flying loose
from its pins, like stray wool on barbed wire.
I know already what the sound track will be:
a smoky flute breathing that ghost of a march
you're conducting right now with a fag-end.

Your wry smile gives me the green light –
the mouth's hallmark curve, your own mother in it –
a glimmer of my *Ga*, and *her* mother – *your Ga* –
Viking quines, their lineage folding back through time
beyond the rainbow on today's horizon,
invisible women in my wide-angle frame,
as you step away up the road's incline;
and yet – there they are, in the jaunt of you,
that quiet defiance, happed in classic tweed
breaking loose from buttons in a careless dance.

Cut to close-up: a shadowed interior – my lens drinks
the silver of your window-lit hair, then tilts
down the neck's white flow, rests
on the brae of your shoulder, blue linen pleats
tailored with grace, like the years you've gathered.

There's so much to see and hear in you – so many layers,
like the constantly shifting shells at Bay of Skaill;
a gurgling burn of word-play in your eyes,
on your tongue – your own kennings coined
for grandbairns' delight; and always the skylark
and wind in your hearing, even between four walls.

Closer still: your thumbs and fingers
unveil a boiled sweet; slow pincer-moves
left and right, right and left (life here
has shown you ambrosia moments won't
be hurried), till the cellophane bud blooms,
and you slip its nectar between your teeth.

Wide shot – exterior: leaning into your spade,
you turn the earth; garden blossoms wag
in the breeze; the girl in you obliges by giving me a birl,
then you settle into a sunlit book;
ritual and rhythm in all your days as they blow
through each season, drawing to a close
on this Northern rim of the world.

A Megan Boyd Fishing Fly for Prince Charles, July, 1981

Megan Boyd, born Surrey, 1915, moved to Brora as a child, where she spent her adult life alone in a cottage without electricity; died in Golspie, 2001; awarded the British Empire Medal; widely regarded as the greatest fly tyer in the world, receiving orders from all over the globe.

My creator has such delicate hands,
in spite of her manly bearing:
her finger tips slip the silver twist
around my tag, then top my tail
in golden pheasant breast feather, and a veil
of Indian crow; wax thread winds and binds me
slow, and I grow as the light wanes
at her window; the North Sea's weight
sweeps the bay in constant counterpoint
to her gentle breath, no pause in her labour's rhythm,
unless to put a match to paraffin or candle
in this hushed and shadowed dwelling;
now black herl, then bend from the stem,
tinsel rib and floss of Maribou Red,
long hackle of folded Chinese yellow,
my body orange and gold,
and at my throat indigo jay to snare
even the most wise among salmon;
with my wing of Bronze Mallard, teal and Red Macaw
I'll be a fitting gift for the bride groom prince,
my jungle cock eyes discerning and true
as any aristocrat's; and – mark this –
I'll endure long beyond the sad,
sweet catch he's already made.

Maggie's Centre, Edinburgh, Tells of Its Conception and Growth

Maggie Keswick Jencks, born Dumfriesshire, 1941, died of breast cancer, London, 1995; writer, artist, garden designer and co-founder of Maggie's Centres – drop-in centres offering free support to anyone diagnosed with cancer. The first Maggie's Centre opened in Edinburgh in 1996; many have since been built across the UK and abroad, designed by the world's great architects, all located adjacent to hospitals.

Washed up on a plastic seat
in a hospital corridor with no horizon,
clutching a cup of lukewarm tea,
is the last place you'd want to be,
fathoming the fact that the thing
you still find hard to name has spread –
tiny jack boots stamping tell-tale tracks
across your liver, bones and marrow,
up and down the ladder of your spine,
your days so suddenly falling away;
she thought she'd paid her dues –
surrendered a breast to this secret army
that multiplies itself without warning,
had even come to like her battle-scarred
Amazon other half. Anonymous and numbed,
in this dead-end tunnel of her worst fear,
she imagined me, the way dark imagines light.

She had me all laid out before she died,
team assigned, my elevations mapped
on paper sheaves festooned about her bed;
and now I'm here, for anyone who needs me,
a place apart where you would want to be.

My sister cells spring up across the globe –
a multiplying matrix; our kitchen table
offers gentle harbour; garden shadow-play
filters light through tranquil fields of glass;
and when bare stalks conceal all signs of Spring,
our curves will hold you close.

Kantha Sari Heirloom

Mina Ray, born Calcutta, 1938, died Kilbarchan, 2013; linguist, community education worker, interpreter, scholar, cultural activist and ambassador; pioneered an empowerment programme of literacy, citizenship and rights issues for women in Greater Glasgow in the 1970s; one of Scotland's first interpreter trainers.

Folded with ritual care, then packed away,
I've been carried over borders drawn by careless men,
from Dhaka to Delhi, and Calcutta in between,
across continents to Scotland, where now I rest,
waiting for occasions to be worn by peerless Mina-di.

My quilted silken stitch, intricate as her intellect,
depicts jasmine and lily – uncommon blossoms
in this stone-grey place, named for an Irish saint –
the village she now calls home; its silent walls
echo with a memory of looms –
nine hundred at the Empire's height.

Like Mina-di – glittering scholar and daughter
of medics to the mogul – I am, among saris,
what we call First Class First, back in Bengal,
but unlike her, I won't renounce my Brahmin caste –
I never could be an everyday item, trauchling to and fro
to Glasgow in the rain – such service falls
to my synthetic siblings – no less elegant
in practical rayon, for Mina-di glides
in every fold she wears, blazing a trail
with pragmatism, that wise third eye
under its scarlet bindi lid, the hallmark
of her teaching, infusing women with self belief:
desh in her book gives nation another meaning,

one without borders, where immigrants and refugees
through a second language may find the weave
of two tongues doubly rich;

and meanwhile, I'm ready when occasion calls,
to be tradition bearer, honoured to drape myself
about my Mina's petite powerhouse form;
and when the moment comes,
to be passed on.

Note: The suffix 'di' added to Mina's name is a term of respect.

Orkney Recalls Gunnie

Gunnie Moberg, photographer, born Gothenburg, Sweden, 1941;
lived most of her life in Orkney, where she died, 2007; described
herself as a Swedish Orcadian; one of twenty prominent Scottish
artists commissioned to produce work for display in the Scottish
Parliament.

It was love at first sight, even though
I warned her with spindrift, then threw
the whole Beaufort Scale at her, lashed
those Viking cheekbones, thrashed
her wheatfield hair into mayhem
and stung her lazulite eyes
with ice pellets, rain and spray –
took her breath away –
but she only laughed and claimed
that every nook and granite cranny,
each sandstone cleft and salt wave,
all the sky and seascapes I can conjure in a day,
the totality of me, was her very element.

Her brightness won me every time –
beguiled me into the perfect light
for my geometry to shine. No-one
had seen me this way before,
from five hundred feet, her lens poised
at the pilot's shoulder, coaxing me
to give my best side; or close up,
at our most intimate trysts,
when she roamed my shoreline geology,
finding the woman in me;
and I laid myself bare for her, always.

The Living Mountain Addresses a £5 Banknote

Nan Shepherd, born Peterculter, 1893, died Aberdeen, 1981; novelist,
poet and writer of non-fiction, lecturer in English at Aberdeen College
of Education; her non-fiction work, The Living Mountain, *written*
in 1941 but not published till 1977, describes the Cairngorms; first
woman to appear on a Royal Bank of Scotland banknote, 2016.

You cavorted through my corries, capered about my braes,
careened between my coiling clouds, played
hide-and-seek on my plateau, glinted as you skipped
across my ruffled secret loch – a butterfly, I thought –
a Silver-studded Blue brought back from extinction;
till the wind dropped, and you came to rest,
snagged in moss campion – a plastic rectangle
pulsing on the tail of a breeze.

I dislike litter, especially your kind – polymer particles
that issue in blizzards from careless markets, slip
from pockets, won't perish in rain or melt with snow;
though in your case, I'll make an exception, because
you bear her face: the woman who never rushed
to my summits, but walked into me, took time to learn
my every line – schist, gneiss and granite – and heard
my braided voice. You've brought her to light again,
all I contain, nurture and sustain, held in her steady gaze.

Rose Stalks in Snow

After a painting by Christian Small, water colourist, mainly self-taught; born Dundee, 1925, died West Linton, Scottish Borders, 2016; graduated with honours in chemistry at the University of St Andrews; sold very few of her many paintings, preferring to give them away; stored sheaves of them in her children's old cot.

My lines mark absence,
the long lack, when sap lies low
and only thorns show;

footprints my presence,
recorded ephemera
on yesterday's snow.

White fills in blank space,
telling tales of buried things;
silence – no bird sings.

Hoarfrost-wizened leaves
cling to withered tendrils, chilled
remnants in stilled air.

At eyeline's corner,
edging my monochrome frame,
faded berries stain.

Though this season numbs,
I'll bide my time till Spring's core
calls colour from the store.

Tessa Thinks the Scottish Poetry Library

Tessa Ransford, OBE, born Mumbai, 1938, died Edinburgh, 2015;
poet, editor, translator, activist, and founder of the Scottish Poetry
Library, the only – as far as is known – purpose-built, independent
public poetry library in the world.

I didn't exist, till, at Festival time,
a visitor to the capital asked her where I was,
and in that one beat, her thought created me,
the *future now*:

a space for poetry and people to tryst
on three foundation stones of language –
Gaelic, Scots and English, a glimmer of syllables
signalled from spines, bound sheaves murmuring distillations,
an infinite exchange of the world's flickering lexicons,
bearing light from centuries' vaults, outward and home again,
thumbed, leafed and loved, cross-fertilised, the way she'd learned
from her Scottish-Indian roots, whose shoots
branched across horizons
into the *future now*.

Poetry goes through walls, she wrote,
and took that thought to the road,
driving our bus from home base,
my store to be shared, poems fluttering
like flags all along the hairpin bends
of Scotland's rugged map,
always reaching, reaching out,
into the *future now*.

Note: *Future Now* and *Poetry Goes Through Walls* are poems by Tessa.

Epilogue

In Memoriam

For Catriona White, teacher, 1951–2015, Edinburgh, and over a thousand stitchers – almost all women – of The Great Tapestry of Scotland.

A friend bid me to her sister's last farewell –
a woman I hadn't known, but her singular tale
was told at the gathering – how she quietly gave
to many. Her voice wove through a recorded choir,
anonymous, mingling with the air we breathed,
as we listened and learned of a legacy; music
in her fingers too, that stitched the image
of a lass with hair like summer corn fields,
bowing a glowing cello in our nation's tapestry;
a butterfly has just alighted on her lifted elbow,
enthralled for one eternal moment,
breathing the nectar of melody, its wings
stilled by the eloquence of women's work.

Scots Glossary

Aa – all
Ablow – below
Abuin / abune – above
Aff – off
Afore – before
Aftentimes / aft-times – often
Agate – on the way, about, around
Agin – against
Aheid – ahead
Ahint – behind
Aiblins – perhaps
Ain – (one's) own
Aince – once
Airm – arm
Airn – iron
Airt – direction, place, quarter
Alane / aa ma lane – alone, all alone
Alowe – on fire
Amang – among
An – and
Ane – one
Anely – only
Appen – open
Auld – old
Awa – away
Awmaist – almost
Awthing – everything
Aye – always
Bainished – banished
Bairns – children
Bane – bone
Bane-thrang – bone-crowded
  (of a graveyard)
Bangster – a bully
Barefit – barefoot
Barrie – fine, excellent

Baurs – bars
Beek – bask
Beelin – boiling
Beir the gree – win the prize
Berkin – barking
Bide – live, stay
Bield – nest
Biggit – built
Beuk – book
Biled / bilers – boiled / boilers
Birlin – spinning, twirling
Bittie – little bit
Blawed – blew
Blen – comfortable
Blin – blind
Bluid – blood
Bowk – retch
Braes – slopes, hillsides
Braig – a challenge
Brainch – branch
Braith – breath
Braw – beautiful / fine / handsome
Breenge – to rush in, to dash in
Breist(s) – breast(s)
Brewster – man in charge of the ale-
  house, publican, brewer
Bricht – bright
Brocht – brought
Brock – left-overs, scraps of food
Broo – brow
Brunt – burnt
By-ordinar – extraordinary
Carl – warlock
Cauld – cold
Caum – calm
Caunle – candle

Cavie – cage
Chap – to knock, rap
Chaumer – chamber
Cherm – charm
Chitter – shiver
Claucht – caught
Cloot – a cloth
Clure – batter, beat
Coont – count
Coorse – course
Couldnae – couldn't
Craik – creak
Cruisies – oil lamps
Croon – crown
Cuddie – a small horse
Cuif – a fool
Daith – death
Darg – daily work
Dauner – stroll
Daurk – dark
Daur – dare
Dawin – dawning
Deid – dead
Dern – secret
Dicht – wipe
Dinna – don't
Dirdum – a racket, an uproar
Dirl, dirlin – ring, ringing (as on stone)
Docht – strength
Dochter – daughter
Dominie – school teacher
Doo – dove
Douce – gentle, sweet
Douk – dip, bathe
Doukers – swimming costume
Dounfaw – bucketing rain
Dowie – sad
Drap – drop
Dreepin – dripping

Dreid – dread
Droon – drown
Droukit – drenched
Dug – dog
Duimster – hangman
Dule – grief, sorrow
Dunt – hit, a blow
Dwaum – dream
Een – eyes
Efter – after
Efternuin – afternoon
Eldritch – ghostly, weird
Embro – Edinburgh
Emerant – emerald
Emerant Isle – Ireland
Ettled – tried
Fae / frae – from
Falderals – fussy frills
Fash – fuss, fret
Faulds – folds
Faur – far
Fecht – fight
Fell – cruel, harsh
Ferlie – wondrous
Fidderin – fluttering
Fissle – tingle
Fit-dunt – footprint
Flair – floor
Flane – arrow
Flee – fly
Flichter – flutter
Flooers – flowers
Fouterin – trifling
Fower – four
Fowk – folk, people
Fund – found
Furrit – forward
Gaen – gone
Gaither – gather

Gear – belongings
Ghaists – ghosts
Gies – gives
Glaum – grab, snatch
Glent – glint
Glister – glitter
Gloamin – dusk
Goon – gown
Gowan – daisy
Gowd / gowden – gold / golden
Greet – cry
Gress – grass
Grun – ground
Grup – grip
Guid – good
Gyte – mad, crazy
Hae – have
Hale – whole
Halse – neck
Hantle – a fair amount
Hapshackled – shackled
Happit – wrapped
Hauf-lit oor – twilight
Hauns – hands
Haurd – hard
Hecht – promise
Heeze – hoist, heave
Heich – high
Heidit – headed
Heiven – heaven
Herm – harm
Hersh – harsh
Hert – heart
Heuch – whoop
Hingin – hanging
Hinner-end – the final portion
Hinnie – honey
Hirple – hobble
Hoast – cough

Hoochmagandie – copulation
Hoose – house
Howk – unearth
Howp – hope
Humph – to carry a heavy burden
Hus – has
Ile – oil
Ilka – each, every
Insteid – instead
Intil – into
Jaurs – jars
Jaups – splashes (of water)
Jeely – jelly
Jizzen – child-bed
Juist – just
Jyle – jail
Jyned – joined
Ken / kennin – know / knowing
Kirtle – dress, gown
Kist – chest
Kyte – stomach
Laithly – loathsome
Lang-kent – long known
Lauch – laugh
Leal – loyal
Leam – to shine, a bright glow
Lear – learn; also teach
Learn ye – teach you
Leet – list
Leid – lead (metal)
Leuk – look
Licht – light
Lik – like
Lippen tae – trust
Lowp – leap
Lowse – release, loosen
Luif – palm (of hand)
Lunnon Toon – London Town
Ma – my

Maik – match, equal, companion
Mair – more
Mairch – march
Mak – make
Makker – Maker (as in God)
Marra – a marriage partner, mate
Masel – myself
Maun – must
Maut – malt
Meir – mare
Melldin – mixing, blending
Merk – mark
Mindin – memory
Misdout – misdoubt
Mitherin – mothering
Mort-kist – coffin
Muckle – much (ower muckle –
    too much)
Mune – moon
Murther – murder
Myntit – intended, meant
Nae – no
Naelstring – umbilical cord
Nane – none
Needit – needed
Nicht – night
Nieve – fist
Niver – never
Nocht – nothing
Noo – now
Nor – than
Norrie – a notion
Oan – on
Ony – any
Ootby – outside
Oor – our / hour
Ower – over
Paiks – punishment, dues
Paised – poised, balanced

Parritch – porridge
Pech – to pant, a breath
Peyed – paid
Pint – point
Plowter – splash, flounder
Polis – police
Pooer – power
Pow – crown of the head
Pyne – pain
Quaich – a shallow drinking-bowl
Quate – quiet
Quine – woman
Raip – rope
Rauzit – gashed
Reek – mist, like smoke
Reeshle – rustle
Reid – red
Richtly – rightly
Reive – plunder
Rig-bane – back-bone
Roon – round
Rowth – abundance
Ruisit – praised
Sab – sob
Saft – soft
Sair – sore
Sall – shall
Samin – same
Sang – song
Sark – shirt
Sauchs – willows
Saucrit – sacred
Sauf – safe
Saul – soul
Saut – salt
Scance – appraise, examine
Scraich – screech, scream
Scaldies – non-travellers
Scaudin – scalding

Scaur – scar
Sclim – climb
Sconce – to mock
Scove – dive
Scrievin – writing
Shouthers – shoulders
Shrood – shroud
Siccar – stable, secure
Siller – silver
Simmer – summer
Sin syne – since then
Skailin – tumbling
Skimmer – flicker
Skinklin – sparkling
Slaw – slow
Slock – to drink deep
Smoor – smother
Snaw – a square-rigged sailing ship
   (can also mean snow, as in weather)
Snawdraps – snowdrops
Sneddin – cutting, slashing
Sneist – to sneer
Sookit – sucked
Sooth – South
Souch – sigh
Spang – stride
Spreet – spirit
Spreid – spread
Stairtit – started
Stane – stone
Stang – sting, pang
Staun – stand
Steikit – stuck, shut
Sterns – stars
Stieve – stiff
Storm-steidit – detained by bad
   weather
Stotter – stumble, stagger
Stott, stottit – rebound, rebounded

Stourie – dusty
Stowen – stolen
Straeberries – strawberries
Strang – strong
Stravaiged – roamed
Stoondin – stunning (with a blow)
Suld – should
Swallin – swelling
Swaw – waves, the swell of the sea
Swelt – sweat
Sweir / swuir – swear / swore
Syne – then
Syped – seeped
Tae – to
Tak – take
Tak tent – pay attention / take note
Tatterwallop – ragged
Tawse – leather belt for corporal
   punishment
Teuk – took
Tint – lost
Thae – those
The day – today
Thegither – together
Thirled – tied, bound
Thocht – thought
Thole – endure
Thrang – a crowd, busy
Thrapple – throat
Threap / threapin – nag / nagging
Threid – thread
Threit – threat
Tirlin – vibrating
T'ither – the other
Tocher – dowry
Tousie – dishevelled
Towe – rope
Traivelled – travelled
Trauchled – weary with toil

Treisures – treasures
Troke – barter, exchange
Twa – two
Unco – strangely, peculiarly
Vaige – voyage
Vyce – voice
Waas – walls
Wag-at-the-waa – a pendulum clock
Wame – womb
Wandert / wannert – wandered
Wanlit – washed out
Wap, wappin – swipe, swiping,
  a violent strike
Warld – world
Warse – worse
Warstled – wrestled
Wather – weather
Watter – water
Waucht – a deep breath of air
  or draught of liquid
Wey – way
Whan – when
Whaes – whose
Whaur – where
Wheen – several
Whilk – which
Whup – whip
Wi – with
Wids – woods
Win – reach
Winnock – window
Wis / wisnae – was / wasn't
Wrang – wrong
Wraith – a ghost, an apparition
Wrocht – wrought
Wull – will
Wund – wind
Wunna – won't
Wurd – word

Yaised – used
Yalder – yell
Yare – eager, keen
Yestreen – yesterday
Yird – earth
Yon – that
Yont – beyond

Gaelic Glossary

Brochan – porridge
Cho brèagha – so beautiful
Corran – a sickle
Machair – coastline grassy plain
Maighread – Margaret
nam Mallachd – of the Curses /
  the Accursed
Ploc – a sod (of peat)
Sgarbh – cormorant

Further Reading

General

Anderson, James, *Ladies of the Covenant* (Bibliolife, 2002).

Craig, Maggie. *Damned Rebel Bitches: The Women of the '45*
(Mainstream Publishing, 1997).

Ewan Elizabeth, Innes, Sue, Pipes, Rose, and Reynolds, Sian (eds),
The Biographical Dictionary of Scottish Women (Edinburgh
University Press, 2006).

Harrower-Gray, Annie, *Scotland's Hidden Harlots and Heroines:
Women's role in Scottish society from 1690–1969* (Pen and
Sword Books Ltd, 2014).

Leneman, Leah, *The Scottish Suffragettes* (National Museums of
Scotland, 2000).

Livingstone, Sheila, *Bonnie Fechters: Women in Scotland 1900–1950*
(Scottish Library Association, Motherwell, 1994).

Strang, Alice (ed.), *Modern Scottish Women: Painters and Sculptors,
1885–1965* (National Galleries of Scotland, 2015).

Swift, Helen Susan, *Women of Scotland* (Creativia, 2016).

Taylor, Barbara, *Eve and the New Jerusalem: Socialism and
Feminism in the 19th Century* (Virago, 1983).

Walker, Charles (ed), *A Legacy of Scots: Scottish Achievers*
(Mainstream Publishing, 1988).

Specific

BRUNTON, MARY

McKerrow, Mary, *Mary Brunton – the forgotten Scottish novelist*,
with foreword by Fay Weldon (Orcadian Ltd, 2001).

Brunton, Mary, *Self-Control* (Pandora Press, 1986).

GARDEN, MARY

Garden, Mary, and Biancolli, Louis, *Mary Garden's Story* (Michael
Joseph 1952).

HUTCHISON, ISOBEL WYLIE

Hoyle, Gwyneth, *Flowers in the Snow – The Life of Isobel Wylie Hutchison* (University of Nebraska Press, 2001).

Wylie Hutchison, Isobel, *North To Rime-Ringed Sun* (Blackie and Son, 1934).

HUTTON, ISABEL EMSLIE

Hutton, Isabel Emslie, *Memories of a Doctor in War and Peace* (Heinemann, 1960).

INGLIS, ELSIE

Leneman, Leah, *Elsie Inglis: Founder of battlefront hospitals run entirely by women* (National Museums of Scotland, 1998).

JACOB, VIOLET

Jacob, Violet, *Tales of My Own Country* (Kennedy and Boyd, 2008).

Anderson, Carol (ed.), *Flemington* by Violet Jacob (Association of Scottish Literary Studies, 1994).

JUNOR, ELIZA

Slaves and Highlanders: Highland Scots in Guyana before Emancipation: http://www.spanglefish.com/SlavesandHighlanders/index.asp?pageid=222591

Slavery: A real piece of the Highlands' heritage, by David Alston: http://www.inverness-courier.co.uk/News/Behind-The-Headlines/Slavery-mdash-a-real-piece-of-the-Highlands-heritage-3977.htm

KESWICK JENCKS, MAGGIE

Keswick Jencks, Maggie, *A View From the Front Line* (Maggie Keswick Jencks, 1995).

Keswick, Maggie, *The Chinese Garden* (Frances Lincoln, 2003).

MACFARLANE, HELEN

Black, David, *Helen Macfarlane* (Lexington Books, 2004); includes Macfarlane's original translation of the Communist Manifesto.

MACMILLAN, CHRYSTAL

Kay Helen, *Chrystal Macmillan: From Edinburgh Woman to Global Citizen*

www.unive.it/media/allegato/dep/n18-2012/Ricerche/Monografica/08__Kay.pdf

MACPHERSON, MARY (MAIRI MHÒR NAN ÒRAN)

Macrae Shaw, Liz, *Love and Music Will Endure – a novel based on the life of Màiri Mhòr nan Òran* (Islands Book Trust, 2013).

Meek, DE, *Màiri Mhòr nan Òran: Taghadh de a h-Òrain* (Comann Litreachas Gàidhlig na h-Alba, 1998)

MELVILLE, ELIZABETH

Reid Baxter, Jamie (ed.), *Poems of Elizabeth Melville, Lady Culross* (Solsequium, 2010)

MOBERG, GUNNIE:

Moberg, Gunnie and Mackay Brown, George, *Stone* (Kulgin Duval and Colin Hamilton, 1987).

NAIRNE, LADY (BARONESS CAROLINE OLIPHANT)

Rogers, Rev. Charles (ed.), *Life and Songs of the Baroness Nairne, with a Memoir and Poems of Caroline Oliphant the Younger* (Charles Griffin and Co, 1872).

RANSFORD, TESSA

Ransford, Tessa, *Not Just Moonshine: New and Selected Poems* (Luath Press, 2008).

Ransford, Tessa, *A Good Cause* (Luath Press, 2015).

SHAW, MARGARET FAY

Shaw, Margaret Fay, *From the Alleghenies to the Hebrides* (Birlinn, 2008).

Shaw, Margaret Fay, *Folksongs and Folklore of South Uist* (Routledge and Kegan Paul, 1955).

SHEPHERD, NAN

Shepherd, Nan, *The Living Mountain* (Canongate, 2011)

SLESSOR, MARY (AND JANIE ANNAN SLESSOR)

Hardage, Jeanette, *Mary Slessor Everybody's Mother: The Era and Impact of a Victorian Missionary* (The Lutterworth Press, 2010).

Robertson, Elizabeth, *Mary Slessor* (National Museums of Scotland, 2001).

SOMERVILLE, MARY

Somerville, Mary, *Personal Recollections, from Early Life to Old Age, of Mary Somerville* (Filiquarian Publishing, originally by John Murray, London, 1874).

STEWART, ENA LAMONT

Stewart, Ena Lamont, *Men Should Weep* (Samuel French, 1983).

SULTER, MAUD

Sulter, Maud, *Passion (Urban −) Discourses on Blackwomen's Creativity* (Urban Fox Press, 1990).

As a blackwoman: poems 1982–1985 (Urban Fox Press, 1990).

TAIT, MARGARET

Neely, Sarah (ed.), *Margaret Tait: Poems, Stories and Writings* (Fyfield Books, 2012).

Neely, Sarah, *Between Categories: The Films of Margaret Tait* (Peter Lang, 2016).

WRIGHT, FRANCES (FANNY)

Morris, Celia, *Fanny Wright: Rebel in America* (University of Illinois Press, Illini Books, 1992).

Index of Quines

Scotland Football Team, 1881:

Hay, Ethel; Osborne, Bella; Wright, Georgina;
Rayman, Rose; Stevenson, Isa; Wright, Emma;
Cole, Louise; St Clair, Lily; Riweford, Maud;
Balliol, Carrie; Brymner, Minnie   71

Luath Press Limited

committed to publishing well written books worth reading

LUATH PRESS takes its name from Robert Burns, whose little collie Luath (*Gael.*, swift or nimble) tripped up Jean Armour at a wedding and gave him the chance to speak to the woman who was to be his wife and the abiding love of his life. Burns called one of the 'Twa Dogs' Luath after Cuchullin's hunting dog in Ossian's *Fingal*. Luath Press was established in 1981 in the heart of Burns country, and is now based a few steps up the road from Burns' first lodgings on Edinburgh's Royal Mile. Luath offers you distinctive writing with a hint of unexpected pleasures. Most bookshops in the UK, the US, Canada, Australia, New Zealand and parts of Europe, either carry our books in stock or can order them for you. To order direct from us, please send a £sterling cheque, postal order, international money order or your credit card details (number, address of cardholder and expiry date) to us at the address below. Please add post and packing as follows: UK – £1.00 per delivery address; overseas surface mail – £2.50 per delivery address; overseas airmail – £3.50 for the first book to each delivery address, plus £1.00 for each additional book by airmail to the same address. If your order is a gift, we will happily enclose your card or message at no extra charge.

Luath Press Limited
543/2 Castlehill
The Royal Mile
Edinburgh EH1 2ND
Scotland
Telephone: +44 (0)131 225 4326 (24 hours)
Email: sales@luath. co.uk
Website: www. luath.co.uk